BRECON BEACONS
A Walkers' Interpretation Guide

Upper part of Sgwd Isaf Clun-gwyn

BRECON BEACONS
A Walkers' Interpretation Guide

by
Andrew Davies & David Whittaker

CICERONE PRESS
MILNTHORPE, CUMBRIA, UK

© Andrew Davies and David Whittaker
First Published 1995
Reprinted 1999

ISBN 1 85284 182 6

A catalogue record for this book is available from the British Library

Dedication
*Dedicated to our families and friends
who have shared this area with us
and especially to Tim.*

Acknowledgements

Special thanks are due to Jean Davies for transcribing many of the cassette tapes made whilst walking the routes, to David Davies for producing the finished diagrams and to Dorothy Whittaker for patient forbearance during long evening hours of writing.

We would like to thank the National Museum of Wales, publisher of *Studies in the Origin of the Scenery of Wales I - The River Scenery at the Head of the Vale of Neath,* for permitting us to adapt Dr F.J.North's diagrams on the geological formation of the waterfalls and on Craig-y-Ddinas and Bwa Maen.

We would like to express our gratitude to the Merthyr Tydfil and District Naturalists' Society, publisher of *The Historic Taf Valleys, Volume Two. In the Brecon Beacons National Park* by John Perkins, Jack Evans and Mary Gillham, for their kind permission to adapt their diagram on the glacial activity in the head of Nant Crew.

Thanks are due to Richard Preece, the Countryside Council for Wales Reserve Warden for the Brecon Beacons National Park National Nature Reserves, for his informative comments on the routes that pass through Craig Cerrig-gleisiad and Craig Cwm-du. Help was also received from the Brecon Beacons National Park Authority who clarified some rights of way.

Front Cover: The Beacons from Cefn-Cantref Farm

CONTENTS

ROUTE	START

Section A North-Eastern Valleys and Ridges

Appendix

ADVICE TO READERS

Readers are advised that whilst every effort is taken by the authors to ensure the accuracy of this guidebook, changes can occur which may affect the contents. A book of this nature with detailed descriptions and detailed maps is more prone to change than a more general guide. New fences and stiles appear, waymarking alters, there may be new buildings or eradication of old buildings. It is advisable to check locally on transport, accommodation, shops etc. Even rights of way can be altered, paths can be eradicated by landslip, forest clearances or changes of ownership. The publisher would welcome notes of any such changes.

Location Map of the Brecon Beacons

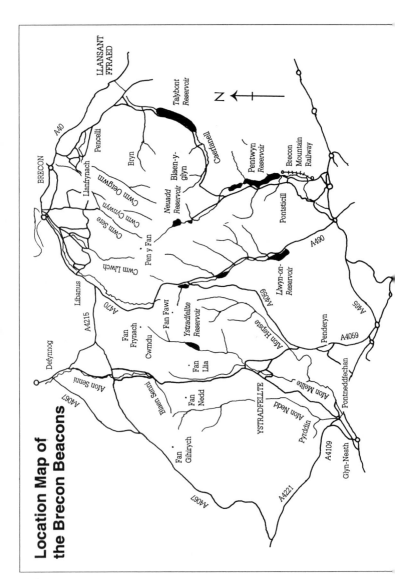

INTRODUCTION

All the walks described in this guidebook are covered by the Brecon Beacons National Park Central Area Outdoor Leisure Map 11. The idea for this book came from a realisation that many walkers in the Brecon Beacons wish to know more of the countryside they come to enjoy and explore. One solution is for them to join one of the many guided walks organised by the Brecon Beacons National Park Authority. Park wardens who lead such events have commented that they are so popular that as many as a hundred people may join a single ramble. This is not only a logistical problem for the warden, but the sheer numbers destroy the wilderness quality of a walk in the countryside with little chance of seeing undisturbed wildlife.

Another approach is a "guided walk" with a difference. A walk guided by a book which tells all the interesting facts that a walk with an expert would provide but still retains the magical wilderness feeling of an isolated mountain summit or the tranquillity of a river ramble. This guidebook has the added advantage of giving information on all aspects of the countryside, as though the walker were accompanied by several experts at the same time.

All the route descriptions are accompanied by a commentary on every aspect of the countryside, including geomorphology, hydrology, geology, botany, zoology, ecology, ornithology, archaeology, local history, land-use and environmental issues. The guidebook is designed to be used by all ages and does not assume that a visitor has any previous mountain walking experience or countryside knowledge.

The description of the walks may be seen by some to contain excessive detail, but we have catered for all abilities. The entry to some of the valleys and the paths in the Waterfall Country require careful route finding. We must emphasise that you should not venture into the high peaks without the knowledge to use both map and compass and without the proper equipment.

All the walks have been explored completely by the authors and have been walked a number of times to check information. The Brecon Beacons National Park Authority are continuously adding signposts and occasionally redirecting rights of way. Features such as Forestry Commission conifer plantations are also changing daily as much of the timber stock in the National Park has reached maturity. As a result, some of the route directions may have changed slightly since publication. The main structure of the walks will, however, have remained as we have described them.

We believe that this is the first guidebook of its kind to the central area of the Brecon Beacons National Park. It is intended for use by visitors on long or short stay holidays as well as by those visiting on a daily basis. The number and variety of walks provides ample scope for repeated visits and even the serious walker would require some considerable time to exhaust the guide completely.

EDUCATIONAL ROLE OF THE GUIDE

A key method of alleviating detrimental effects resulting from the use of the countryside by the public is by informal education - a relatively new concept which is becoming ever more apparent to countryside managers. Over the past decade or so, the number of people visiting the Brecon Beacons National Park has risen significantly. This has resulted in numerous conflicts of interest, both concerning nature conservation and with the farmers who depend on this area for their livelihoods. These conflicts can be greatly reduced by increasing the environmental awareness of visiting users. An educated user is also likely to be sympathetic and supportive of the objectives of the National Park and may possibly take an active role in promoting these aims.

A dilemma faced us in writing this guide - will an increase in walkers in previously low intensity used areas destroy the very reason for attracting them there in the first place? We feel that an increase in visitors is inevitable in the long term. As routes such as the Pont ar Daf path to the summit of Pen y Fan have become overcrowded, visitors have overspilled into other areas in an attempt to experience undamaged wilderness. This has resulted in conflicts with nature conservation and farmers.

Access is largely within the control of the Brecon Beacons National Park Authority. In fact, the number of visitors is fortunately limited by car parking space. Hopefully, the publication of this guidebook will result in an environmentally sensitive user so helping to reduce conflicts in the Brecon Beacons National Park.

HOW TO USE THE GUIDE

The guidebook is divided into five geographic sections with a number of routes in each:

- A.   Brecon Beacons - **north-eastern** valleys and ridges
- B.   Brecon Beacons - **eastern** valleys and ridges
- C.   Brecon Beacons - **south-western** valleys and ridges
- D.   Fforest Fawr
- E.   Waterfall Country

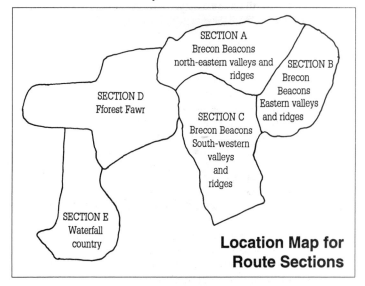

SECTION A
Brecon Beacons
north-eastern valleys and ridges

SECTION B
Brecon Beacons
Eastern valleys and ridges

SECTION D
Fforest Fawr

SECTION C
Brecon Beacons
South-western valleys and ridges

SECTION E
Waterfall country

Location Map for Route Sections

This guidebook must be used in conjunction with the Brecon Beacons National Park Central Area Outdoor Leisure Map 11. A total of 33 routes are described with a number of alternatives and extensions giving further variety. Low level and high level routes of different lengths and degrees of difficulty are included to cater for all weather conditions and ability.

All the routes are designed to:
- Be circular
- Include as few roads as possible
- Be easily completed in a morning/afternoon

- Require only basic map and compass skills
- Be interesting, exploring little frequented areas
- Be within the scope of all age groups
Each route has a basic format:

1. Title of walk, letters A to E indicate geographical area. See general location map p.11.

2. Grid reference of the start, distance and height gained. Turn to the Appendix for instructions on how to find the start of each route. The glossary will help you to translate place names. See below on how to find a grid reference.

3. An introductory section gives a brief description of the walk, its difficulty and its main points of interest.

4. You will find that the route itself is divided into numbered highlighted sections that are clearly marked on the sketch map. These bold sections are differentiated from descriptive material to facilitate clear and easy navigation in adverse conditions.

5. **Alternatives** to the route make a detour and rejoin at a later section. **The point at which the Alternative leaves the main route is noted in the main text but the description of the Alternative comes at the end of each walk.**

6. **Extensions** to the route are of two types: they either have to be reversed to rejoin the main route at the point at which it was left or they are a circular extension. **The point at which the Extension leaves the main route is noted in the main text but the description of the Extension comes at the end of each walk.**

7. You will find information boxes within each route and these describe points of interest that are common to a number of routes.

8. References are frequently made to information boxes that are found within other routes e.g. Maen Llia, see D5.

9. Annotated sketch maps are given for each route.

FINDING A GRID REFERENCE

All the routes in this guide are to be found on the 1:25,000 scale Outdoor Leisure Map of the Brecon Beacons National Park Central Area. On this scale 1cm on the map represents 25,000cms or 250 metres on the ground. The grid lines on Ordnance Survey maps are 1km apart and it is a useful estimate that the diagonal of the grid is about 1.5km.

All the grid lines are numbered so that each square on the map can be identified by quoting the numbers relating to the two lines bounding the square on the bottom and its left-hand side (west). An eight figure grid reference is used to define a location on the map. For example GR 0123 2158 can be used to identify the position of Pen y Fan. From the diagram below, one can see that the number corresponding to the grid line running along the bottom of the box is given first followed by the number corresponding to the grid line running vertically along the left-hand side of the box. An easy way to remember which figure comes first is that you have to go along a corridor before going up the stairs.

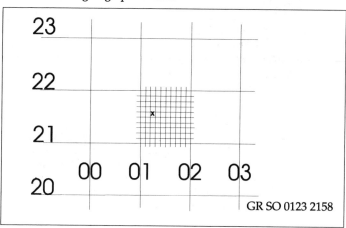

GR SO 0123 2158

CHOOSING A SUITABLE WALK

The table on page 16 will help you in choosing something suitable for the day and your mood. The various categories of difficulty are on an

Cwm Llwch Cottage with Corn Du

increasing scale from 1 to 5. All distances quoted are taken from the map but the real distance may be increased by at least 20% depending on height gained. Problems of route finding are noted along with an assessment of the steepness of the terrain. A high score in the Bad Weather column indicates that the route becomes much harder whereas a low score in this column means that the route is not affected by poor weather. A fit mountain walker will not find any of the routes particularly strenuous.

Particularly interesting categories of features that can be seen on the walk are also scored on an increasing scale from 1 to 5. For example, if you are particularly interested in archaeology, scanning down this column will reveal that routes E1 to E4 score highly.

Once you have chosen a suitable walk from the table, you will find it described in miniature in the introductory box at the beginning of each route.

Some of the valleys, especially the northern ones, offer a multiplicity of routes. We have not sought to be exhaustive, but our intention has been to choose walks using all the ridges in such a direction as to present the best unfolding panorama. Valleys have been included to give shorter, less strenuous walks or as an alternative in bad weather when all but the most adventurous might eschew the high places.

ROUTE	DIFFICULTY						
	LENGTH	HEIGHT GAINED	BAD WEATHER	STEEPNESS OF ASCENTS & DESCENTS	EXERTION	ROUTE FINDING	SUITABILITY IN BAD WEATHER
A1	4	5	4	4	4	3	N
A2	4	5	4	4	4	3	N
A3	1	2	2	1	2	1	Y
A4	4	5	4	4	4	3	-
A5	4	4	4	4	4	3	-
A6	4/5	4/5	4	5	4/5	3	N
A7	1	2	2	1	2	1	Y
A8	3	4	4	4	3	3	-
A9	3	4	4	3	3	3	-
A10	4	4	5	4	4	3	N
A11	2	2	2	1	2	1	Y
A12	3	3	4	4	4	4	-
A13	5	3	4	4	4	2	-
A14	5	3	4	2	4	4	N
A15	1	1	1	1	1	2	Y
B1	1	2	2	2	2	2	Y
B2	3	3	3	3	4	3	N
B3	3	3	3	2	3	2	Y
B4	3	3	3	2	3	2	Y
B5	4	3	4	3	4	3	N

INTEREST						
GEOMORPHOLOGY (GLACIAL)	GEOLOGY	BIRDS	FLOWERS	WATERFALLS	PANORAMAS	ARCHAEOLOGY
5	3	4	5	2	5	3
4	3	3	5	-	5	3
5	2	4	4	2	-	-
5	4	3	4	-	5	4
3	4	3	4	-	4	-
5	4	2	4	-	4/5	4
2	3	3	2	-	-	-
3	3	4	3	-	4	1
3	2	4	2	-	4	1
4	3	3	2	-	4	1
2	2	2	2	-	-	1
2	2	4	3	1	5	4
2	2	4	3	1	5	1
2	2	3	2	-	5*	1
2	2	3	3	1	-	1
2	1	2	2	-	5	-
2	2	2	2	-	4	2
3	3	4	3	3	5	-
3	3	4	3	4	5	-
3	3	3	2	1	5	1

ROUTE	DIFFICULTY						
	LENGTH	HEIGHT GAINED	BAD WEATHER	STEEPNESS OF ASCENTS & DESCENTS	EXERTION	ROUTE FINDING	SUITABILITY IN BAD WEATHER
C1	5	4	4	3	4	2	N
C2	3	3	5	2	3	4	N
C3	3	4	4	3	3	3	N
D1	1	2	2	3	1	1	Y
D2	3	3	4	1	2	4	N
D3	2	3	3	1	2	3	-
D4	4	3	4	1	4	3	N
D5	3	2	3	1	2	3	-
E1	1	-	1	1	1	1	Y*
E2	5	-	1	2	4	2	Y*
E3	4	-	1	2	3	2	Y*
E4	4	-	1	2	3	2	Y*
E5	4	-	1	1	3	2	Y*

INTEREST						
GEOMORPHOLOGY (GLACIAL)	GEOLOGY	BIRDS	FLOWERS	WATERFALLS	PANORAMAS	ARCHAEOLOGY
4	3	3	3	-	5	3
2	2	2	2	1	2	-
3	3	2	2	1	3	-
4	3	5	5	-	2	1
3	2	2	2	-	4	-
3	3	5	5	-	3	3
4	3	5	5	-	3	3
2	2	1	2	-	5	2
2	4	4	4	4	-	5
2	5	5	4	5	-	5
5	5	5	4	5	2	5
5	5	5	4	5	-	5
5	5	5	5	5	-	2

PHOTOGRAPHIC HINTS

Compared with some of the more rugged mountainous regions of Britain, the Brecon Beacons do not have many striking photographic compositions. This is mainly because the summits and ridges are gently rounded and interesting rocky foreground, which lends depth and perspective to a scene, is rarely found.

The northern valleys in Section A are very difficult to photograph from the valley floor as they are often in shadow. This lighting problem is exacerbated in winter. The north-east faces of the summits catch the sun as it rises above the ridge but this only lasts a short while and the faces are soon in shadow for the rest of the day. The summit of Pen y Fan is a good vantage point for taking photographs in almost every direction. The eastern valleys and ridges in Section B are well lit by a morning sun as they face to the south and east but an early start will find the best angled light and deepest colours. In contrast, the south-western valleys of the Brecon Beacons (Section C) are only lit in the afternoon.

The spectacular crags of Craig Cerrig-gleisiad are invariably in shadow and only catch a very early morning sun whereas Craig Cwm-du faces in the opposite direction and is illuminated late in the afternoon or evening. An early start after a snowfall late in the season will, however, be rewarded with the crags beautifully lit.

The waterfall area of Ystradfellte is so well wooded, and has such deep gorges, that lighting in the valley floors can be rather poor. Rivers and waterfalls pose special problems. High shutter speeds will "freeze" the movement of the water but give a rather static unnatural appearance. Longer exposures allow small lens apertures to be used giving greater depth of field and imparting a "cotton wool" appearance to moving water. Be careful as this effect can be overdone with very slow shutter speeds.

For these reasons, we have gone to some length to suggest good viewpoints for photographs and even, on occasions, describing suitable foreground material. Those walkers who are far more experienced in photography than ourselves will forgive us for being patronising, but those with less skill will perhaps find these notes useful.

In general, the best times for taking pictures are early or late in the day, but the geography of the high summits makes it extremely difficult to capture sunsets with the peaks silhouetted against a striking sky. Sunsets from the summits themselves are a different matter but require very careful framing to include interest in the foreground. However, some of the most spectacularly atmospheric mountain pictures can be taken just before or after a heavy storm at any time of the day.

We have largely used slide material (Kodachrome 64 ASA or Velvia 50 ASA) for the colour pictures in this guide. These are rather slow emulsions but they produce high definition pictures. For landscapes it is usually important to have maximum depth of field and the majority of our work has entailed using a tripod. Monochrome pictures were usually taken using Ilford XP2 or FP4 film.

We have chosen to use 35mm cameras for ease of transportation, accompanied by prime lenses of 28mm, 50mm and 135mm focal lengths, plus zoom lenses within the 28mm to 80mm focal length range. Camera bodies were Contax, Leica and Pentax.

Since we have sought to capture the natural environment, we have used only skylight or UV filters and, in the case of monochrome shots, occasionally orange filtration.

Many of our pictures were taken either against the light or in snow conditions. In these circumstances it is important to override automatic metering by opening up the lens iris by half to one stop to avoid underexposure.

Landscape photography is often seen as being straightforward in comparison to, say, portraiture or still life. In fact this is not the case and attention to a number of important factors will pay dividends:

- Always try to include close-up features in the foreground to add depth to your pictures.

- For silhouettes try to use sunset light, ideally reflected in a pool or lake. Meter off the brightest part of the scene but bracket your exposures as well.

- Use any focal length of lens for the best effect. Many landscape photographers prefer 28mm or shorter but remember that close-ups of walkers or rock shapes produce very striking effects.

- Apertures should usually be f16 or smaller to produce maximum depth of field but special effects of differential focus require wide apertures. Ideally your camera should have depth of field scales or a preview button.

- For colour pictures use a slow emulsion for good saturation and fine grain. Sunlight or a sunbeam for splash of colour is best. For monochrome pictures a slow fine grain emulsion gives good detail.

- Filters are a matter of choice and some landscape photographers use a whole range from graduated through colour tints to polarising. We prefer natural light but have used graduated grey or blue to darken skies and give good exposure in darker foregrounds.

- The horizon should be set either above or below the centre of the frame otherwise a poorly composed shot is usually the result.

- Shutter speeds in fractions of a second should not be less than the focal length of the lens in mm for hand-held pictures. For example, 1/30th sec for 28mm lens and 1/250th sec for 250mm lens.

- Pictures are best taken with a tripod and small apertures.

- For good composition try to get "leading lines" into the picture. These can be walls, rivers, tracks, ridges or rock formations.

- Be patient. Study the scene and maybe return several times to get the best lighting. Different times of day and season may produce much better pictures.

GLOSSARY

Aber	River mouth
Aderyn	Bird
Afon	River
Allt	Wooded
Aran	High place
Bach	Little or small
Ban, Bannau	Peak or crest
Blaen	End, point, top, head of
Bod	Dwelling
Bont	Bridge
Bryn	Hill
Bwlch	Pass
Cadair	Chair
Cae	Field
Caer	Fort, stronghold
Canol	Middle
Capel	Chapel
Carn/Carnedd	Cairn or heap
Carreg	Stone or rock
Castell	Castle
Cau	Hollow
Cefn	Ridge
Celli	Grove, copse
Cemaes	River bends
Cerrig	Stones
Cilfach	Corner, nook
Clawdd	Hedge or ditch
Clog	Crag, cliff
Clogwyn	Cliff
Clun	Meadow
Clydach	Torrent
Clyn-gwyn	White meadow
Coch	Red
Coed	Wood
Comin	Common
Craig	Rock/cragg
Crib	Combe/sharp ridge
Cribin	Rocky ridge
Croes	Crossroads
Cwar	Quarry
Cwm	Valley
Cymmer	Meeting of rivers
Ddinas	Fort
Dol	Meadow
Drws	Door
Du, ddu	Black
Dulais	Dark stream
Duwynt	Windy
Dwfr, dwr	Water
Dyffryn	Valley
Eglwys	Church
Eira	Snow
Esgair	Ridge
Fach	Peak
Fan	Peak or crest
Fawr	Great or large
Fechan	Smaller
Felin	Mill
Fford	Road
Ffynon	Spring/well
Foel	Rounded bare hill
Gallt	Wooded hill
Garn/garnedd	Cairn/heap
Garth	Hill
Glas	Blue/green
Gleisiad	Young salmon
Glyn	Valley
Goch	Red
Gwaun	Moor

Gwladus .... White lady
Gwyn/gwen ... White
Gwynt .... Wind
Hafodydd .... Summer
                 dwellings
Hebog .... Hawk
Hen .... Old
Heol .... Road
Isaf .... Lower
Llan .... Village/church
Llech .... Flat stone/slate
Llithrig .... Slippery
Llwch .... Lake
Llwyd .... Grey, brown
Llyn .... Lake
Maen .... Stone/block
Maes .... Field/meadow
Melin .... Mill
Melyn .... Yellow
Moel .... Rounded/bare
                 hill
Mynydd .... Mountain
Nant .... Stream
Neuadd .... Hall
Newydd .... New
Ogof .... Cave
Pant .... Hollow, valley
Pentre .... Village,
                 homestead
Penyr .... End of or Top of
Perfedd .... Middle
Pistyll .... Spring, waterfall
Plas .... Hall, mansion
Pont .... Bridge
Porth .... Gateway
Pwll .... Pool
Rhaidar .... Waterfall
Rhiw .... Hill/slope

Rhos .... Moorland
Rhydd .... Ford
Sarn .... Causeway, old
                 road
Sgwd .... Waterfall
Sticill .... Stile
Sych .... Dry
Twll .... Hole
Twyn .... Hill
Uchaf .... Upper, highest
Waun .... Moor
Wen .... White
Y, Yr .... The
Y Groes .... Crossroads
Y Pannwr .... The Fuller
Yr Eira .... Snowy
Ystrad .... Valley floor

North-Eastern Valleys and Ridges

CWM LLWCH

A1. Cwm Llwch/Cefn Cwm Llwch

Start:	Llwynbedw, Cwm Llwch
Grid Reference:	0062 2455
Distance:	9.5km (6 miles)
Height Gained:	620m (2035ft)

This is a fine route into the most westerly of the northern Beacons valleys and it progresses in a southerly direction into the valley head below the north face of Corn Du - the second highest peak in the range. The walk goes up the stream in the valley floor to a corrie lake. There are good waterfall views overshadowed by the looming bulk of Corn Du. It then works its way up the right (W) ridge and so up to the summit of Corn Du. From here it continues over to the summit of Pen y Fan (the highest peak in the Beacons) and returns to the start via the ridge, Cefn Cwm Llwch. An alternative shorter route returns to the start from the obelisk below Corn Du, dropping down Pen Milan ridge on the west of the valley. The final climb to the summits is steep, as is the upper part of the descent from Pen y Fan. Route finding is straightforward in good weather, but in mist or winter conditions ability to use compass and map is important. The walk requires a reasonable degree of fitness. Interest factors include the geomorphology of the area, plants and birdlife, waterfalls and lake, good panoramic views and archaeological features.

* * *

ROUTE
1.   **Start at the end of the car park where there is a 'NO MOTORS' sign. The ford and the hillside on the left of the car park is your descent. Follow the track leading into the valley, lined with beech, hawthorn, mountain ash and hazel.**

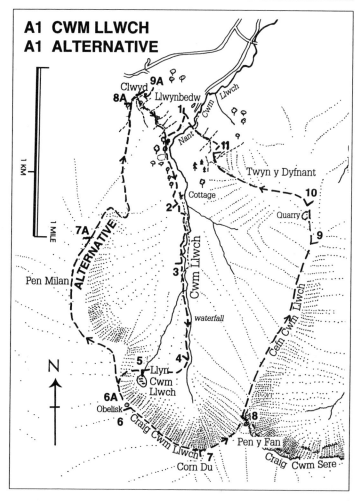

The woodland on the right contains the poorly preserved earthworks of an Iron Age hill fort which is marked on the map as a dotted oval and labelled "Settlement". This is a small enclosure with widely spaced ramparts. Its value as a hill fort is dubious as although the land slopes away east to Nant Cwm Llwch, the land to the west and south rises gradually to the foot of Pen Milan.

The track soon comes to another ford across the same stream, Nant Cwm Llwch, with a wooden bridge on the left, through a second gate and then between wooded banks with fields on either side. From here there are good views into Cwm Llwch with waterfalls in the foreground and a backdrop dominated by Corn Du straight ahead and Pen y Fan on the left.

The track continues southwards between old stone walls and then detours around Cwm-llwch Cottage.

Notice the abundant ferns and mosses on the sloping roof of an outhouse on the northward facing end of the cottage.

Leave the cottage on your left and skirt around the right of the farmyard by crossing over two stiles.

2. **The wide open track ahead takes a direct line up a spur of land with stream courses on either side. However, this line is of little interest and avoids the superb waterfalls glimpsed earlier. Descend instead to the left and walk along the fence which soon reaches the stream. Here a small track crosses to the left bank although either can be followed to the waterfalls.**

This is a most interesting habitat as, after the birch woodland is left behind, the banks of the stream are lined with closely grazed grassy areas where there are many different species of wild flowers, such as lousewort *(Pedicularis sylvatica)*, bird's-foot trefoil *(Lotus corniculatus)*, red bartsia *(Bartsia odontites)* and eyebright *(Euphrasia sp)*.

Notice that the valley slopes have a high density of hawthorn trees - a notable feature of Beacons valleys. For this reason, the number of bird species is more typically associated with a woodland than an open valley. Keep a sharp lookout for tree pipit, green finch, redstart, wren, whinchat, yellowhammer and chaffinch. Even the great-spotted woodpecker has been recorded. Do not be surprised to see green woodpeckers often far from trees where they feed on ants. The falls and stream bed are good places to spot grey wagtail, heron and dipper.

The valley is unusual in that there are two stream beds which have eroded the floor leaving a raised spur of land in the centre

(Geology and geomorphology of Cwm Llwch, see A3).

3. The hill fence crosses the stream ahead but there is a low level stride over it just before the stream divides. The left branch of the stream is the more interesting and just ahead is an impressive waterfall. This can be climbed on the right arriving first at a small pool above the lower fall.

The falls are shaded by a mixture of hawthorn, blackthorn, ash, rowan, willow and silver birch. Most of the trees are young or have grown from previously fallen trunks. Luxuriant bryophytes and ferns thrive on damp and wet rock faces surrounding the fall. Ferns include the rare Wilson's filmy fern *(Hymenophyllum wilsonii)* and *Cystopteris fragilis*. Bryophytes include *Ulota crispa, Mnium undulatum, Hylocomium splendens, Atrichum undulatum, Neckera pumila, Fissidens taxifolius, Philanotis fontana, Hyocomium armorica, Frullania tamarisci* and several others. Several ungrazed tall herb ledges can be seen to the left and right of the fall. Interesting vascular plant species include valerian *(Valeriana officinalis)*, wild angelica *(Angelica sylvestris)*, meadow sweet *(Filipendula ulmaria)*, *Alchemilla vulgaris*, wood avens *(Geum rivale)* and Welsh Poppy *(Mecanopsis cambrica)*.

Climb up the right side of the upper fall reaching a series of smaller waterfalls from where there are magnificent views of Corn Du.

Surprisingly, the flat-topped summit of Corn Du at the head of valley falsely appears higher, from this view point, than its neighbour, Pen y Fan, which is on the left.

4. When the stream starts to break up into many smaller tributaries, leave the stream to the right, striking westwards to the corrie lake of Llyn Cwm Llwch.

Flushed areas at the head of the valley are extensively covered in soft rush *(Juncus effusus)*. Llyn Cwm Llwch is a good place to have a break and appreciate this special place (Mythical Connections; Geology and Geomorphology of Cwm Llwch; Glacial Origins of Llyn Cwm Llwch, see A3).

5. Take the path which leads to the right (W) up the steep slope in a zigzag, climbing steeply to the lower end of the ridge of Craig

Cwm Llwch, near to the Tommy Jones Obelisk, a useful landmark in poor visibility (GR 0005 2175).

The path has been severely eroded into a deep gully, firstly by the passage of feet which destroyed the protective turf, and now by a combination of walkers and water. It becomes a watercourse in heavy rain.

Looking back down to the left from the obelisk is a fine view of the hummocky mounds of glacial moraine that dam the lake of Llyn Cwm Llwch.

A1 Tommy Jones Obelisk - The obelisk is a memorial to Tommy Jones, aged five, who died here in 1900 of exhaustion. He was attempting to walk alone from Cwm Llwch farm to the Login. It now serves as a useful landmark in poor visibility by marking a rapid descent route from Cefn Cwm Llwch to the safety of the valley below ensuring that walkers today do not suffer the same fate.

** ALTERNATIVE ROUTE LEAVES FROM HERE **

6. Follow the ridge of Craig Cwm Llwch (SE) up the steep slope to the summit of Corn Du.

Severe footpath erosion has occurred here, resulting in a wide scar all the way from the obelisk to just below the summit. After a wet spell the ground becomes very soft, with little grass remaining. Originally the turf bound the soil together but once this protective covering was destroyed, soil and stone were rapidly transported downhill by the passage of booted feet. Remedial work by the National Trust has done a great deal to stabilise this area and there are encouraging signs that in the future it will recover, leaving only the mark of a man-made path constructed of natural stone.

From Craig Cwm Llwch you may see buzzard, carrion crow and raven wheeling overhead. Ravens nest nearby on the crags of Craig Cwm Sere. You will undoubtedly see or hear meadow pipit and skylark as they are the commonest birds over hill grasslands. If you are especially observant you may see ring ouzel as they breed in the vicinity of the crags. This area is near to the limit of their British range.

The final 10m or so to the summit of Corn Du involves scrambling up the Plateau Beds but a stepped path leading diagonally right will avoid further damage to these loose crags.

Pen y Fan from Corn Du in winter

An interesting path-come-sheep track avoids this and cuts East across the northern face of Corn Du below the crumbling cliffs of Plateau Beds to the col leading to Pen y Fan (Geology of Brecon Beacons, see C1).

The crags are covered in grazed purple moor grass heath (*Vaccinium*). Awnless sheep's fescue (*Festuca vivipara*) is the only plant species of interest.

From the top of the stepped path cross left (E) to the summit of the crags overlooking Cwm Llwch.

7. From the cairn follow the crags (E) and descend into the col. The path swings around (ENE) and climbs along a broad track, well marked by cairns. The final one is of Bronze Age origin and leads to the trig point on the summit of Pen y Fan.

Pen y Fan at 886m (2906ft) is the highest mountain in South Wales and just fails to achieve "Munro" status, a term given to summits over 3000ft. For a description of the mountain and its panorama see A2

(Photographic compositions from Pen y Fan) and see A5 (North-east face of Pen y Fan).

A1 Pen y Fan vista - The summit of Pen y Fan is one of the finest vantage points in Wales. On an exceptionally clear day, Cadair Idris can just be distinguished to the north and Exmoor to the south. Fforest Fawr to the west possesses many interesting features and is a relatively unvisited part of the park. Almost due west are the cliffs of a beautiful glacial cwm, Craig Cerrig-gleisiad. To the south-west the plumes from the stacks of Port Talbot and Llandarcy can be seen on a clear day and in between these is the wide sweep of Swansea Bay which culminates in the west with the Mumbles Lighthouse.

---

8. **Scramble carefully down the crags due north of the summit cairn and follow the ridge of Cefn Cwm Llwch for about 2km.**

As you scramble down from the summit, look carefully at the upper surfaces of the near horizontal Plateau Beds for ripple marks. These are also present on the surfaces of rocks making up the summit. They were formed in exactly the same way as ripples are formed in the sandy beds of rivers today. Look back at the north-east face of Pen y Fan where in early spring you can see the brilliant colours of rare arctic-alpines (see A4).

Looking back (SSW) up the ridge there is a panorama forming an attractive subject for a photograph using Cefn Cwm Llwch with Cribyn on the left, Pen y Fan just right of centre and Corn Du to the right.

9. **Take a small path which leaves the main track and bears left (N) towards the pile of stones at the disused quarry of Cwar Mawr (GR 018 236).**

10. **From here descend WNW (292°) to the spur of Twyn y Dyfnant and down the steep slope to the hill fence, keeping to the right of the coniferous forestry.**

11. **Cross the fence through a gate (GR 0091 2411) and follow the line of trees diagonally down the slope. An indistinct path leads**

Exploring the upper reaches of Cwm Du *(Routes D3 & D4)*
Sgwd Gwladus from the western bank *(Route E1)*

North-east face of Pen y Fan from Cwm Sere *(Routes A4 & A5)*
Reflections of north-east face of Pen y Fan in a pool on Bryn Teg
(Routes A5, A6 & A8)

directly down the field after 80m. Head for the junction of hedges to the left and continue down the slope to the ford across the stream (GR 0067 2440) and back to the start of the walk.

** ALTERNATIVE ROUTE **
Follow Sections 1-5 of Route A1.

6a. From the obelisk turn north and follow the footpath which swings first right, left, then right again around the head of a side valley of Cwm Llwch, with steep slopes on the right. Just before the final spur of Pen Milan, the path changes into a broad green old quarry track.

The hill vegetation comprises dwarf shrub heath and grass heath in which ling (*Calluna*) and bilberry (*Vaccinium myrtillus*) are common. Purple moor grass (*Molinia caerulea*) is abundant on flatter areas.

7a. The route descends to the right diagonally across the valley side.

This track has obviously seen heavy use in the past and, in fact, was used to transport Old Red Sandstone (see B3) from a quarry on the left, now abandoned. The softer rock was used as road infill, whereas the harder stone was used in building.

The quarry track swings sharply right and then left, descending between grassy banks and heading due north again. The path becomes ill-defined in places but eventually the fences on either side funnel the path to a gate.

8a. Pass through the gate, ford a small stream, and follow the tree-lined track to the yard with the cottage of Clwydwaunhir on the left.

9a. Opposite the house is a small ford and a stile. Cross these and cut across some fields (SE) back to the start of the walk.

A2. Cwm Llwch Ridge Walk

Start:	Llwynbedw, Cwm Llwch
Grid Reference:	0062 2445
Distance:	10km (6 miles)
Height Gained:	620m (2035ft)

A high level circuit of Cwm Llwch involving ascents of the two highest mountains in South Wales, Corn Du and Pen y Fan. The walk follows a horseshoe, climbing the Westerly ridge to the high summits and descends the Eastern ridge along the route described in A1. The ascent is gentle at first but the final climb to the summit of Corn Du and the descent from Pen y Fan are steep. In good weather, route finding presents no problems but will certainly require the use of map and compass in poor weather. The walk requires reasonable exertion. The main interest features are the geomorphology, the birdlife and the superb views from the summits.

* * *

ROUTE

1. **Start from the car park in a field at the end of the track from Pont Rhydybetws. There is a sign NO MOTORS'. Continue along the main track into the valley of Cwm Llwch. After about 200m there is a wooden waymark sign on the right. Take the path to the right and follow up the hill into the field. The path goes past deciduous woodland with alder trees on the left and comes to a stile near a large oak tree. Continue in a north-westerly direction, reaching a second wooden stile with yellow waymark arrows and then head towards a renovated farmhouse, turning right to bypass it on your left.**

Looking back, and to the south, you can see into Cwm Llwch valley. On the right is the bulk of Pen Milan over which this route climbs.

Skirting round the farm buildings cross a stile and the field ahead to a house in the trees (Clwydwaunhir). Cross a stile and walk down the left of the hawthorn hedge to a stile and stream. After crossing the stream, turn sharp left and follow the sign to Pen Milan.

2. **Continue between holly trees, fording the stream again and**

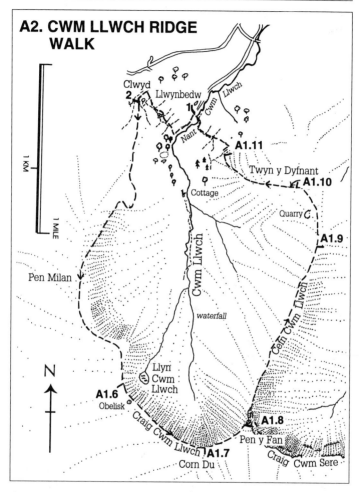

A2. CWM LLWCH RIDGE WALK

follow the track ahead to the gate with yellow waymark arrow and the National Trust sign to Pen Milan. This is where you cross the hill fence.

3. Head due south along an indistinct path aiming for the left side

of the spur of land ahead and following the land grooves up to the crest. A slightly sunken grassy track leads diagonally up the valley side to a path through gorse and bracken.

From here look left up the valley to Pen y Fan on the left and Corn Du on the right. Far over to the east is Cefn Cwm Llwch ridge which will be your descent route. The route drops down this ridge to Twyn y Dyfnant to the square outline of a Forestry Commission plantation. The descent route is on its left (N) edge. Down in the valley is Cwm Llwch cottage below the waterfalls, which are visited by routes A1 and A3.

Pass a group of hawthorn trees on the left and follow the old quarry track to a point where it swings sharply back to the right at the first zigzag.

The track has raised borders and at the point where it swings back to the left you have a good view north over the Brecon Valley.

Continue south between small quarry spoils and keep on the main track to a flattened area of quarry debris. From here follow a walkers' path to the cairn and through peat haggs to a broader section of the ridge and so to the obelisk.

For further details of the origin of this monument see Route A1.

From this landmark **Route A1 is joined at point 6** and this is followed to the summits of Corn Du and Pen y Fan, finally descending the ridge of Cefn Cwm Llwch, so completing the circuit of this beautiful valley. If the weather has deteriorated, a quick descent can be made from the obelisk down an obvious path to Llyn Cwm Llwch below. It is an easy walk back down the valley to the start.

A2 Photographic compositions from Pen y Fan - Good compositions for photographs are numerous - wide-angle shot north-north-east with Cwm Llwch in the centre, Cwm Llwch left and Cwm Sere right; west from the north-east corner of summit of Corn Du left, Llyn Cwm Llwch and the Fans; south-south-east of Neuadd Valley using crags on eastern face of Pen y Fan as foreground; east of Cribyn; wide-angle shots north-east of Cribyn, Beacons ridges and Black Mountains.

A2 Corn Du - This is the site of a Bronze age cairn and the stones near the edge are the remains of an excavated funerary mound (also see Cairn Pica, B2). Corn Du is a fine vantage point with views to the west of the Fans and, in particular, of the finely sculpted headwall of Fan Fawr to the south-west. In the valley just below to the west is Blaen Taff Fawr, the head-waters of the River Taff. The south-east presents a quite different aspect down into the valley of Neuadd with its reservoirs and continuing view towards the South Wales coast in the distance.

A3. Cwm Llwch Valley Walk

Start:	Llwynbedw, Cwm Llwch
Grid Reference:	0062 2455
Distance:	6km (3.75 miles)
Height Gained:	340m (1115ft)

Cwm Llwch is a beautiful valley leading from the wooded plain south of Brecon and up into the U-shaped glacial upper reaches climbing under the spectacular head wall of Corn Du. This walk is one for a more gentle frame of mind or perhaps when conditions suggest caution in venturing too high on the mountains. No great height is reached but the atmosphere of the Beacons is savoured and the scenery is typical of the northern valleys. An early start is rewarded by the eastern sun lighting not only the valley floor and waterfalls, but also the north-eastern face of Corn Du. The walk is safe in terms of route finding and requires average fitness. Features of interest include the geology and glaciology, the plant and birdlife, waterfalls, mountain scenery and local mythology.

* * *

ROUTE
Follow route A1 to the waterfalls and across to Llyn Cwm Llwch (Sections 1-4).

> **A3 Mythical connections** - Llyn Cwm Llwch had an enchanted island only accessible through a tunnel from the shore. The island rose out of the water only on May Day when fairy flowers could be gathered to fairy music. The flowers were so lovely that a sacrilegious visitor brought some away with him and down the mountain. When they faded, the island disappeared below the waters and has never been seen again.

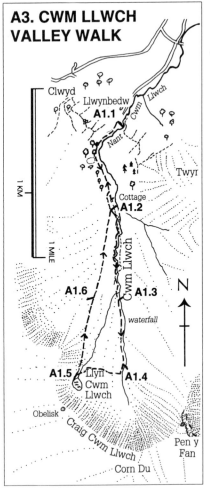

A3. CWM LLWCH VALLEY WALK

Clwyd

Llwynbedw
A1.1

Twyi

Cottage
A1.2

Cwm Llwch

A1.6   **A1.3**

waterfall

N

A1.5 Llyn   **A1.4**
Cwm
Llwch

Obelisk

Craig Cwm Llwch

Pen y
Fan

Corn Du

Walk up the track to Cwm Llwch cottage, by-passing it on the right through the field and over two stiles. The preferred route up the valley is via the waterfalls because height is gained gently and there are opportunities to frame photographs of the hills in interesting foreground.

5. From the northern end of the lake the path heads down the valley on the return walk. Descend to a cairn where the track is joined by the one from Corn Du which zigzags down from above the lake. Continue down on the crest of a spur which divides the valley into two in its upper reaches, gaining a good view of the northern end of Cwm Llwch and the agricultural areas to the north.

6. On reaching the hill fence, cross it by a stile alongside which is a National Trust sign for the Brecon Beacons.

7. This is where the ascent route left the main path and crossed to the stream way earlier in the walk and it is now easy to retrace your steps back to the start.

A3 Glacial origins of Llyn Cwm Llwch - Llyn Cwm Llwch is a small oligotropic corrie lake having a surprisingly shallow maximum depth of only 8m. At a first glance, Llyn Cwm Llwch appears to have been formed by glacial ice sculpting out a deep basin in solid rock but a closer inspection reveals this not to be the case. The shallowness of the lake and the hummocky mounds which surround it are the clues to its origins. The lake is situated at the head of Cwm Llwch in a spot which receives the most shade from the sun. Here, one of the last remaining blocks of ice from the Ice Age lingered on. Rock fragments plucked from the Brownstone crags above by freeze-thaw, a process where water in fissures in the rock freezes, expands, cracking the rock and then melts, penetrating the rock even further before refreezing, tumbled over the wasting ice mass to accumulate in a ring around its edges. When the ice finally melted, a small lake dammed by the ring of moraine was left. This process is the same as in the formation of "kettle-holes" of which a fine example can be found beneath Craig Cerrig-gleisiad.

A3 Geology and geomorphology of Cwm Llwch - Cwm Llwch was carved by glaciers during the last ice ages but its shape is different from many of the other glacial valleys in the Beacons. The upper section is relatively flat and contains a corrie lake, Llyn Cwm Llwch, but the gradient steepens in the middle section where the waterfalls are found before the gradient eases again near Cwm-Llwch Cottage. The reason for this may be a more resistant band of rock which is also responsible for the formation of the waterfalls. The classical U shape of glacial valleys has been further modified in the middle section by two streams which have cut down into the valley floor leaving a ridge which the main footpath follows.

CWM SERE

A4. Cwm Sere/Cefn Cwm Llwch

Start:	Pont y Caniedydd
Grid Reference:	0394 2439
Distance:	9.5km (6 miles)
Height Gained:	560m (1841ft)

This route explores one of the most spectacular and wildest valleys in the Beacons and includes sections which can be demanding in snow and ice conditions. It is a fulfilling mountain walk, the lower reaches of which are well wooded and lead in to an amphitheatre created by the steep northern slopes of Cribyn and Pen y Fan. A mountain stream with small waterfalls creates interesting foregrounds for pictures of Cribyn and Pen y Fan - the two highest peaks in the Beacons. The upper parts of the route can be quite serious in bad or winter conditions but a number of less demanding variations are possible. The ability to read map and compass is important. The main features of interest are the geomorphology and glaciology, the panoramic views and some archaeological sites.

✳ ✳ ✳

ROUTE

1. **From the car parking area at Pont y Caniedydd, cross the bridge and head south up the tarmac road, passing a farm (Bailea) on the way.**

On the right of the road in Cwm Sere is a woodland nature reserve managed by the Brecknock Wildlife Trust (see A7). At the head of this valley is the north-east face of Pen y Fan and to its left is Bryn Teg ridge.

Continue on past the turning on the left to Bailea farm and follow the road up the hill to where it swings sharp left and through a gate.

2. **Ignore this turning and follow the stony track for 250m straight ahead to a gate in the hill fence on the far side of which is a new National Trust sign for Cwm Cynwyn.**

A4. CWM SERE/CEFN CWM LLWCH

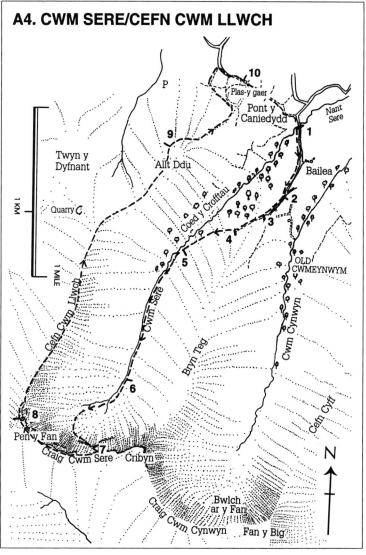

The ridge on the right is the descent route leading towards the end of the walk. The stony track you have just walked along is part of the Roman Road that leads to Bwlch ar y Fan and so is commonly known as the "Roman Road" (see A11).

The Scots pines *(Pinus Sylvestris)* immediately on the left as you cross the hill fence may have been planted by the side of the Roman Road as route indicators to drovers and, if this is the case, would have signalled that shelter and grazing could be obtained from the farm nearby. The Roman Road was probably used long before the Romans or even the Celts came to the Brecon Beacons.

3.   Bear right at the gate and follow the stone wall around the front of Bryn Teg and into the valley of Cwm Sere.

4.   After about 400m the stone wall has collapsed (GR 0330 2336) Just after this point drop gradually across the slope until the streamcourse is reached.

The trees on these slopes can be used to good effect as foreground for pictures of the upper reaches of Cwm Sere.

5.   Follow the streamcourse, either by scrambling along the bank or by staying on more even ground above, following a convenient sheep track.

Small waterfalls in the upper reaches provide good foregrounds for wide angle pictures of the north-east face of Pen y Fan (see A5).

6.   Once in the basin below Cribyn, strike across towards the foot of the north-east face of Pen y Fan and from here climb the headwall by the track which starts from bottom right and continues to top left.

You will cross piles of stones brought down the gullies by the winter frosts. The headwall track rises at an easy angle, presenting no problems, and arrives at the unnamed col between Cribyn and Pen y Fan. There is a good view of Cribyn during the ascent and small crags may be used as suitable foreground to give perspective to a photograph.

7.   From the col, climb steadily (W) following the line of Craig

North-west face of Cribyn from Cwm Sere

Cwm Sere to the summit of Pen y Fan.

Good photographs of Cwm Sere are possible from the col. Just above the col a number of rocks provide foreground interest for a photograph of the north-east face. Such pictures are particularly impressive in winter with icicles hanging from the ledges. In early spring the vibrant colours of rare arctic-alpines may be seen on the most inaccessible crags.

A4 Flora of north-east face of Pen y Fan - This steep, impregnable face protects one of the true botanical treasures in Britain from grazing sheep. The combination of high altitude and a shaded northern aspect create living conditions more akin with polar latitudes than temperate southern Britain. Extensive ledges high up on the face are crammed full of interesting and unusual species which bring the otherwise bleak and foreboding crags alive with vibrant colour in spring. Interesting plants include roseroot *(Sedum rosea)*, rock stonecrop *(Sedum forsteranum)*, mossy saxifrage

---

(Saxifraga hypnoides), purple saxifrage (Saxifraga oppositifolia), vernal sandwort (Minuartia verna), sea campion (Silena maritima), Wilson's filmy fern (Hymenophyllum wilsonii), globe flower (Trollius europaeus), serrated wintergreen, green spleenwort (Asplenium viride), lesser meadow rue (Thalictrum minus), brittle bladder-fern (Cystopteris fragilis) and northern bedstraw (Galium boreale). These ledges also support an unusual collection of bryophytes and several upland invertebrate species including a rare arctic aphid. These plants and animals are highly specialised to be able to survive in these extreme conditions.

As you walk up Craig Cwm Sere, remember to glance back for fine views of the face of Cribyn and down the Neuadd Valley.

Looking back down Cwm Sere from the approach to Pen y Fan, there is an ideal view of its geomorphology. Cwm Sere was carved by ice into a U-shape but this has been altered slightly since the last Ice Age. On the left there is a distinct step in the valley side, a post-glacial feature known as an "antiplanation terrace" while Nant Sere has been eroding away a notch in its base (Glacial Origins of U-shaped valleys see A10).

A4 Antiplanation Terrace - An antiplanation terrace is formed when a snowbed develops on a sheltered step in a valley side. This snowbed erodes into the hillside by freeze-thaw action, depositing material further down slope. In the case of the western side of Cwm Sere, a minor platform was formed due to differences in resistance to erosion of underlying rock types and, in fact, this antiplanation terrace may be related to the change from Brownstones to the underlying Senni Beds (see C1).

Looking up the slope is the flat capped summit of Corn Du and, to the left, is Bwlch Duwynt, which means "Windy Gap". The final ascent to the summit of Pen y Fan is up a very stony area which is rapidly eroding due to the passage of walkers. The National Trust have attempted to build a zigzag path up this face to the top. The crags here are made of Plateau Beds that form a distinctive cap to the summits of Pen y Fan and Corn Du (Geology of Brecon Beacons, see C1).

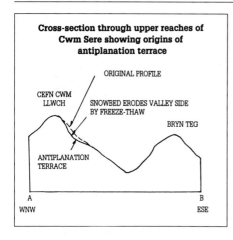

Cross-section through upper reaches of Cwm Sere showing origins of antiplanation terrace

ORIGINAL PROFILE

CEFN CWM LLWCH

SNOWBED ERODES VALLEY SIDE BY FREEZE-THAW

BRYN TEG

ANTIPLANATION TERRACE

A
WNW

B
ESE

Walk across the flat surface of Pen y Fan, which is also badly eroded, to the trig point. This can be found in bad visibility by carefully following the north-east crag line. The trig point is at the end of this to the left.

The north-east face is very steep and care must be taken not to stray too near the edge, especially in strong south-westerly winds or when corniced in winter.

The summit is the site of an Iron Age cairn and there are good views and photographic opportunities from here. For details of the geomorphology of Pen y Fan, see A5. For descriptions of the views to be seen from this, the highest point in the Beacons, see Photographic Compositions from Pen y Fan, A2.

The slope of the summit surface is the key to the dip of the resistant Plateau Beds which cap the summit (Geology of Brecon Beacons, see C1). The summit is, in fact, the dip slope of this rock formation which lies unconformably on the Brownstones but the general trend in dip of all the rock strata in this area is to the south. A slight component of the dip controls the drainage in the valley sides favouring the eastern facing slopes. A close look at the map reveals this to be true for the majority of the gullies in Cwm Sere and Cwm Cynwyn.

8. Leave the summit of Pen y Fan by carefully scrambling NNE down the exposed Plateau Beds. The rocks can be slippery but the route drops quickly to the fine ridge of Cefn Cwm Llwch.

As you scramble down from the summit, look carefully at the upper surfaces of the near horizontal Plateau Beds for ripple marks. These are also present on the surfaces of rocks making up the summit.

45

They were formed in exactly the same way as ripples are formed in the sandy beds of rivers today. Below to the left is the valley of Cwm Llwch (see A3) and the lake of Llyn Cwm Llwch (see A3). Looking down to the right you will see a large gully which holds a frothy white cataract after heavy rain.

Once on the flat section of the ridge, look across to the east for a magnificent view over the ridges of the Beacons and the triangular profile of Cribyn. Looking through the gap between Cribyn and Pen y Fan, you can see the bluff of the ridge which leads down on the right-hand side of the Neuadd Valley. Turning to the entrance of Cwm Sere, there is a pleasant woodland area which is managed by the Brecknock Naturalists Trust (see A7).

Follow the path along the flat ridge, leaving it when it drops gradually to the valley of Cwm Gwdi. Keep to the eastern edge of the ridge, following a path through some boggy areas with mainly heather, past the disused quarries and onwards to Allt Ddu.

As you come to the end of this spur of Cefn Cwm Llwch, which is very well populated with skylarks in spring and summer, there is a good view looking back to Pen y Fan with Cribyn on the left and Corn Du sticking through the gap in the ridge. A pool with rushes in the foreground gives reflections of the hills. As you descend this route further you can see the town of Brecon over to the left beyond the end of the ridge. There is an area of heather and bilberry with the odd pool in the peat. This is one of the best viewpoints of all the peaks in the Beacons and the only place from where you can clearly see the four high summits from the northern valleys. As you come over the end of this ridge, you arrive at a number of hummocks and hollows. These are part of an old quarry and you can look down past a rowan tree growing out of the crags to Cwm Cynwyn Farm. There is a rock outcrop here with bedding showing clearly and the trees and stones on the eastern flank of this ridge provide a number of foreground options for photographs of Pen y Fan and Cribyn.

9. From the pools on the summit of Allt Ddu drop down past the stones of the quarry towards the Plas-y-gaer settlement. Just on the edge of this hill there is a distinctive furrow in the hillside which is an old quarry path. Continue down this path (marked with a dotted line on the map) towards the settlement, descending the

front of the ridge.

The descent of this ridge provides a good view of the Plas-y-gaer settlement with the earth bank being now planted with a line of large trees.

A4 Plas-y-gaer - Plas-y-gaer is an Iron Age settlement some 2000 years old, gaer meaning fortress and plas meaning place. The site is unexcavated but was probably built to defend the surrounding fertile land. There are surviving earthworks forming an oval shape and the height of the main rampart varies between 2 and 3.2m. As there is no sign of an entrance, access was probably gained from the north. No ancient features are visible in the interior.

At the bottom of the slope turn left in front of the settlement. As you come round the corner of the settlement ignore the gate which leads down to a track and continue along a partially built stone wall with a field on the far side. Follow the wall to a gate leading down a track on the line of the trees. This old sunken track is quite overgrown and a small stream runs at the bottom of it, making it easier to walk on the bank.

The track is lined with silver birch, alder, holly, hawthorn and hazel.

A wooden stile leads over onto a farm track. Turn right and head for the Plas-y-gaer buildings. Continue along the track to a gate leading into the farmyard. Turn left then right and left again through another gate.

10. From here head across the field to a line of pylons. To the right of the pylons in the hedge line is a footpath, quite easily seen from here but not evident as you leave the farm buildings. This path leads into the next field and exits it by a gate almost in the top right-hand corner.

A large barn away to your left is the farm of Croftau.

After passing through the gate go down through the valley to another gate which you will see in the field about 60m in front of you. Follow the wire fence on the right-hand side down slope to the derelict buildings. Walk to the left of the farm buildings to a stile in a fence and on to a track. The track you are following has a stone

wall on the left and is open to the field on the right, mainly lined with hawthorn, hazel, rowan and holly. At the end of the farm track is a gate beyond which is a tarmac road. Turn right on the road and drop down the hill to the start at Pont Caniedydd.

A5. Cwm Sere/Bryn Teg

Start:	Pont y Caniedydd
Grid Reference:	0394 2439
Distance:	11km (6.5 miles)
Height Gained:	641m (2103ft)

A classic route from the north side of the Beacons and well worth choosing for a first visit. It includes a superb valley walk with small waterfalls, a climb up the head wall, a detour to the highest peak of Pen y Fan, return via Cribyn and the Bryn Teg ridge. There are good views of the Beacons themselves, the Black Mountains and even of Cadair Idris to the north on a clear day. Route finding, as in all high places, may require map and compass and the final climb to the summits can be hard going. There is particular interest in the geomorphology and some of the best views in the whole of the Beacons.

* * *

ROUTE
1. From the car park turn right (N) along the road for 100m to where it bends to the right (NE) and flattens out at the crest of a hill. Leave the road through a gate taking a track to the left (W). The track leads to Pant Farm after 200m and then curves round to the left in front of the buildings.

Look left (SW) for a good view of the north-east face of Pen y Fan with Cwm Sere in the foreground beyond the trees. On the left is Bryn Teg ridge leading up to the prow of Cribyn. This will be your descent route. On the eastern side of this ridge is the brown scar of the Roman Road running over the Bwlch separating Cribyn from Fan y Big. Looking back the way you have walked, the escarpments of the Black Mountains are visible on a clear day.

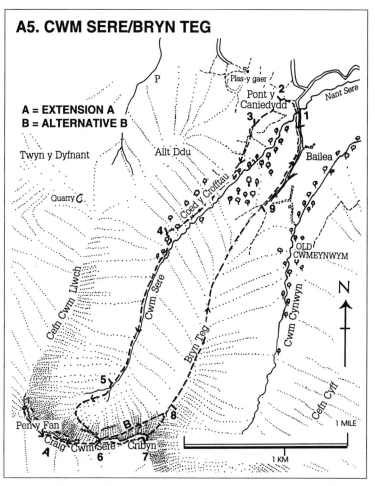

A5. CWM SERE/BRYN TEG

A = EXTENSION A
B = ALTERNATIVE B

2. Continue on this track, leaving the buildings on your right, and climb steadily up the slope through a gap between hawthorn hedges. Bear right and then left, continuing in the direction of Cwm Sere to Croftau.

3. At Croftau the house is apparently inhabited and you should leave it on your left, passing through the metal gate past a large oak on the right and keeping to the left side of the field to another iron gate where you enter Cwm Sere proper.

The woodland on the far side of the stream on your left is managed by the Brecknock Wildlife Trust (see A7).

Continue through yet another gate along the obvious track leading into loose woodland and across to a gap in the tree line. Continue across the field for 300m to a line of trees in front of you. In the centre of this barrier is a gate leading to a track which bears up slightly right past moss covered ant hills and through mixed woodland of beech and hazel.

Deciduous woodland such as this attracts varied birdlife and, depending upon the time of day and season, there is the possibility of seeing woodpeckers and owls as well as other typical woodland species.

The track is easily followed as it drops through the woods

North-east face of Pen y Fan from Cribyn

crossing a small stream running down from the right. At the end of the woodland is the hill fence through which a gate leads out onto hillside opening up a magnificent view of Cribyn on the left and Pen y Fan straight in front.

4.   Drop into the stream bed and follow this upstream, encountering small waterfalls on the way towards the headwall at the end of Cwm Sere between the north faces of Pen y Fan on the right and Cribyn on the left.

You can expect to see dippers in the stream bed and, with luck, a buzzard wheeling overhead or a heron hunting its prey near the water. Cwm Sere was carved by ice into a U-shape but this has been altered slightly by a snowbed eating away at its western side in post-glacial times and by Nant Sere eroding away a notch in its base (Glacial Origin of U-shaped valleys, see A10; Antiplanation terrace, see A4).

5.   Once in the basin below Cribyn strike across towards the foot of the north-east face of Pen y Fan.

The sheer immensity of the north-east face of Pen y Fan can be fully appreciated from the head of the cwm.

A5 North-east face of Pen y Fan - The north-east face of Pen y Fan rises some 380m (1200ft), becoming vertical near the top where the more resistant Plateau Beds form a distinctive cap to the summit. Both units of the Lower Old Red Sandstone, Plateau Beds and Brownstones are well exposed in the face. The ribbed nature of the Brownstones is due to the alternations of sandstone with softer marls. The brown scars on the face of the mountain are testimony to the relentless onslaught of the elements of weather and processes of erosion. The most deadly of these is freezing and thawing of water in cracks in the rocks which literally shatters the stone along existing lines of weakness. The Brownstones are particularly well bedded and cleaved and split apart forming regular blocks, seemingly made for constructing dry-stone walls and buildings. Gravity then plays its part in transporting stone and soil down slope. Rainwater percolates into the ground where it is concentrated along the upper surfaces of the less permeable marly layers. Eventually it seeps out

---

of the face leading to erosion of the soft marls. This undermines the sandstone blocks above leading to their collapse. This water is then concentrated in gullies further eroding soil and rock which is then channelled to the bottom of the face where it spreads out forming talus cones. Look out for a distinctive white, frothy stream which forms in the large gully on the right of the face after heavy rain. In snow and ice conditions, the gullies provide spectacular winter climbing routes for daring climbers using crampons and ice axes. The most difficult section is the final vertical rock band which is extremely exposed and requires a steady nerve, especially if a cornice has formed on the summit which must be tunnelled through, an exhausting feat and a real test of stamina after such a long climb. Unfortunately, the routes are seldom in condition and you will only come across successful climbers on rare occasions. When the cliffs are unfrozen, they are extremely dangerous as the rock is very loose.

From the foot of Pen y Fan take the track up the headwall which starts from bottom right to top left. Crossing piles of loose stones at first, the headwall track rises at an easy angle, presenting no problems, and arrives at the unnamed col between Cribyn and Pen y Fan.

** EXTENSION A and/or ALTERNATIVE B may be followed from here **

6. Turn left (E) up the steep eroded slope to the summit of Cribyn.
The ascent of Cribyn is rewarded with an impressive panorama on a clear day with good views west of the north-east face of Pen y Fan and east of the other Beacons valleys and ridges, Fan y Big and the Black Mountains beyond.

7. Descend (NNE) following the narrow prow of Cribyn.
Just before you start the descent there is a good view north with the ridge of Bryn Teg in the foreground forming the central feature with the valley of Cwm Sere to the left mirrored by Cwm Cynwyn to the right.
The steep descent down the nose of Cribyn can be exciting in snow and ice conditions and may well require crampons and an ice

Ice climbing in the Beacons

axe. Stop now and again to enjoy the views - look over into the adjacent valley of Cwm Cynwyn through which runs the Roman Road (see A11) running up to Bwlch ar y Fan between Cribyn and Fan y Big.

A small pond at GR 0252 2159 provides an excellent opportunity to photograph a reflection of the north east face of Pen y Fan.

8. The return route heads north-north-east down Bryn Teg on a wide grassy track to a wooden gate past a sign reading "Entry to National Trust Land" (Bannau Brycheiniog - The Brecon Beacons).

Other pools and boggy areas further along the ridge provide foreground interest for photographs of Pen y Fan.

9. Follow the stony track (between hedges) which leads down to a crossroads where you take the metalled road ahead. This leads back to the stone bridge from where you started.

The stony track is part of the Roman Road (see A11).

** EXTENSION A **
Climb W along Craig Cwm Sere to the summit of Pen y Fan.

The final ascent of Pen y Fan is badly eroded but the National Trust have built a zigzag path out of the Brownstones to reduce further damage.

Now descend back to the unnamed col between Pen y Fan and Cribyn and rejoin Route A5 at the beginning of Section 6.

** ALTERNATIVE B **
Traverse around the shoulder of Cribyn along a sheep track.

This is the most exciting mountain route in the Beacons, the narrowness of the path and the steep drops giving the walker a real taste of exposure. Remember that great care must be exercised here in winter conditions where crampons and ice axe may well be the order of the day (see A6 for a description of the flora of the north-west face of Cribyn). Look back now and again at the north-east face of Pen y Fan which dominates the skyline, making this one of the finest viewpoints in the Beacons. The final part of this traverse affords grand views of Cwm Sere and across Allt Ddu to the town of Brecon on the left.

Now rejoin Route A5 just above the start of Section 8.

A6. Cwm Sere Ridge Walk

Start:	Pont y Caniedydd
Grid Reference:	0394 2439
Distance:	10km (6 miles)
Height Gained:	560m (1841ft)

This is one of the classic ridge walks in the Beacons. The route climbs the ridge on the east side of the valley and includes ascents of Cribyn and the highest peak in the Beacons, Pen y Fan. Descent is via Cefn Cwm Llwch, the ridge on the west border of the valley. The ascents and descents in the upper reaches are steep and good walking fitness is essential. Interesting features include a nature reserve, the mountain geology and excellent views of all the high peaks and the valleys associated with them.

* * *

ROUTE
1. From the car parking area at Pont y Caniedydd turn SE, cross over the bridge and up the lane ahead.

On the right of the road into the valley of Cwm Sere is a woodland nature reserve managed by the Brecknock Wildlife Trust (see A7).

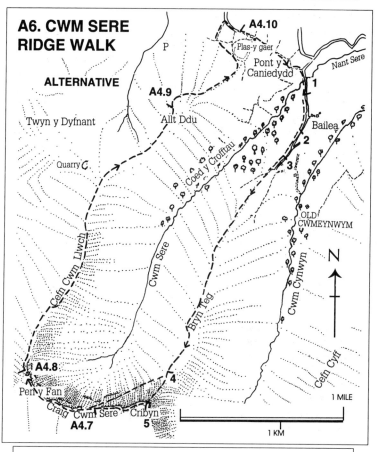

A6. CWM SERE RIDGE WALK

ALTERNATIVE

A4.10

Plas-y gaer

Pont y Caniedydd

Nant Sere

A4.9

Twyn y Dyfnant

Allt Ddu

Bailea

Quarry

Coed y Crofftau

1

2

3

OLD CWMEYNWYM

Cefn Cwm Llwch

Cwm Sere

Bryn Teg

Cwm Cynwyn

Cefn Cyff

N

A4.8

Pen y Fan

Craig Cwm Sere

Cribyn

A4.7

4

5

1 MILE

1 KM

A6 Cwm Sere - Nant Sere drains the vast cauldron formed by the headwalls of Cribyn and Pen y Fan. Water avens and mossy saxifrage grow on the banks of this mountain stream which then flows on through ash, alder and birch woodland. Cwm Sere is extremely rich in flora and fauna with over 200 species of flowering plants and ferns, abundant fungi, birds and insects, at least two of which are rare arctic-alpine species.

Continue past the turning on the left to Bailea Farm, and follow the road up the hill to where it swings sharp left and through a gate.

2. Ignore this turning and follow the stony track, the old Roman Road (see A11), for 250m straight ahead to a gate in the hill fence on the far side of which is a new National Trust sign for Cwm Cynwyn.

On the left is the ridge of Cefn Cyff which leads down from Fan y Big and straight ahead is the ridge of Bryn Teg which you are about to ascend to the summit of Cribyn. On the right is Cefn Cwm Llwch which leads down from Pen y Fan and this will be your descent route.

3. Continuing from this point at the hill fence, ignore the stony track which goes off to the left and head straight for the ridge ahead of you. After a concentrated pull up the beginning of this ridge you arrive at a cairn. The ridge ascends in three main steps and after the second major climb you arrive at a level section marked by a second cairn. The final step is the ascent of the prow of Cribyn.

The step in the middle of the ridge has formed due to the underlying geology. This step is known as a secondary scarp and results from a change from Brownstones to Senni Beds (see C1). The final level section has a number of pools which can be used as foreground for pictures of Cribyn and Pen y Fan. An especially good pool can be found down to your right, just before you begin the ascent of the prow of Cribyn. This provides good reflected images of Pen y Fan.

** ALTERNATIVE ROUTE LEAVES FROM HERE **

4. Carefully climb the narrow path to the summit.

Looking to your left at this point you can see over to the 'gap' with the Roman Road (see A11) passing through it.

5. From the summit of Cribyn descend west along a distinct eroded path to the col.

To the South you look down into the Neuadd Valley where two small reservoirs dam the Blaen Taf Fechan which is fed by surface run-off and ground-water collected in this basin.

You now join route A4. Cwm Sere/Cefn Cwm Llwch at point 7 and follow this back to the start at Pont y Caniedydd.

**ALTERNATIVE ROUTE **
Follow the Cribyn face path off to your right leading to the col between Cribyn and Pen y Fan.

The further you travel, the steeper the cliff becomes with the Brownstones becoming more prominent up to your left. These are responsible for forming the red soil of the path. On a still day you will often hear the sound of croaking ravens high above you. Towards the end of the path, as you cross a number of small gullies, there are quite steep drops away to the right and the path surface becomes uneven and stepped. As you are walking along this path the views of the main face of Pen y Fan change and become even more impressive (North-east face of Pen y Fan, see A5). This path can be dangerous in winter conditions and crampons and ice axe may be needed.

A6 Flora of north-west face of Cribyn - Ledges of this face are more accessible to sheep grazing than those of the north-east face of Pen y Fan and so the interesting arctic-alpine plants are not so prolific. Nevertheless, roseroot *(Sedum rosea)*, mossy saxifrage *(Saxifraga hypnoides)*, purple saxifrage *(Saxifraga oppositifolia)*, and vernal sandwort *(Minuartia verna)* are common. Rock stonecrop *(Sedum forsteranum)* can be found but is more localised. Other species include cowberry *(Vaccinium vitis-idaea)*, green spleenwort *(Asplenium viride)*, brittle bladder-fern *(Cystopteris fragilis)*, limestone bedstraw *(Galium sterneri)*, viviparous fescue *(Festuca vivipara)*, great wood-rush *(Luzula sylvatica)*, cowslip *(Primula veris)*, common wild thyme *(Thymus drucei)* and northern bedstraw *(Galium boreale)*. The wet ledges also support an excellent collection of upland bryophytes.

A7. Cwm Sere Valley Walk

Start:	Pont y Caniedydd
Grid Reference:	0394 2439
Distance:	6.25km (3.6 miles)
Height Gained	250m (820ft)

A low level walk around one of the most beautiful and spectacular of the Welsh valleys. The sheer size and steepness of the impressive

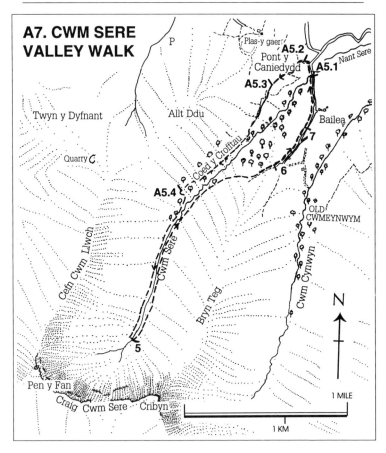

A7. CWM SERE VALLEY WALK

north-east face of Pen y Fan can be fully appreciated from the head of Cwm Sere. Like all the valley walks there is little danger of getting lost even in poor weather and it can be enjoyed with a leisurely approach requiring not too much exertion. The main features of interest are the geological features of the headwalls and north eastern faces, the glacial valleys and the woodlands.

* * *

ROUTE
Follow Route A5 Sections 1 to 4 to the head of Cwm Sere.

5.   **Cross over the stream and make your way down the eastern side of the valley. The going is easier if you keep above the steep-sided stream gully making use of the occasional sheep track. Eventually, the hill fence forces you above the stream and guides you to the gate where you meet the Roman Road.**

6.   **Take the stony track for 250m where you bear left when you meet a metalled road.**

A7 Cwm Sere woodland - The woods on the eastern bank of Nant Sere are leased from the National Trust by the Brecknock Wildlife Trust and 42 acres are managed as a nature reserve. Even though it has been heavily grazed in the past, the majority of the trees appear to be very old. Parts of the woodland are very wet and these areas are dominated by alder. A particularly rich collection of insects, liverworts and fungi thrives in these boggy conditions where rotting wood is abundant. Drier areas of woodland are populated with ash, rowan, cherry, field maple and sessile oak. Brown birch is common near the top of the wood. Woodland birds are numerous and include willow warblers and redstarts with a surprisingly large rookery located in a clump of birches. Open glades in the wood are ideal habitats for species such as pied flycatchers. The reserve has a wide range of invertebrates including a number of specialities such as a rare lace-wing fly and rare craneflies. All in all this reserve is a fascinating area, the combinations of damp and dry woodland and damp and dry glades resulting in a great variety of plant and animal species.

---

7.   **Follow this down the hill and so back to the start just across Pont Caniedydd.**

A7 Woodland birds - Woodland birds include blue tit, great tit, coal tit, pied flycatcher, nuthatch, redstart, tawny owl, green woodpecker, lesser-spotted woodpecker, great-spotted woodpecker, jay, wood pigeon, blackbird, treecreeper and wren. Warblers migrate in summer from southern climes to nest on the woodland floor.

A7 Changing woodland - Trees started to recolonise the Brecon Beacons after the last Ice Age which ended around 12,000 years ago. Arctic-alpine vegetation first established itself which was then invaded by a scrubland of dwarf birch with some juniper. Taller birches and, to a lesser extent, Scots pine, followed. The climate continued becoming warmer and drier and, around 9000 years ago, pine and birch remained on lower hill slopes but the upland was covered in hazel with valleys full of damp oak woodland with lime and elm. Woodland grew much higher than it does today, up to 600m, above which grew alpine grassland. Climatic conditions then became even warmer and humid allowing the formation of blanket peats 7000-5000 years ago. Alder, elm and oak thrived in damp valleys. Drier conditions returned, elm disappeared and beech made its first appearance. The climate started to decline again and has continued to the present. Sessile oak, ash and beech woodland developed and still dominate today.

CWM CYNWYN

A8. Cwm Cynwyn/Bryn Teg

Start:	Pont Caniedydd
Grid Reference:	0394 2439
Distance:	8km (5 miles)
Height Gained:	641m (2102ft)

The route enters Cwm Cynwyn and crosses the stream to the other side of the valley, avoiding the busy and rather monotonous walk along the Roman Road. An ascent of Cribyn via Craig Cwm Cynwyn is followed by an exciting descent along the prow of Cribyn and an easy walk back along Bryn Teg ridge. The headwall ascent to Cribyn and the first part of the descent to Bryn Teg are steep. Adverse weather may make the use of map and compass mandatory and in snow and ice conditions crampons are desirable. The walk is quite energetic. A nature reserve, the glacial nature of the valley, the views from Cribyn and the Roman Road are the main points of interest.

∗ ∗ ∗

ROUTE

1. Cross the bridge and head south up the tarmac road, passing a farm (Bailea) on the way.

On the right of the road in the valley of Cwm Sere is a woodland nature reserve (see A7) and at the head of this valley is the north-east face of Pen y Fan. To its left is Bryn Teg ridge.

Ignore the turning on the left to Bailea Farm and follow the road up the hill to where it swings sharp left and through a gate.

2. Ignore this turning and follow the stony track straight ahead to a gate in the hill fence on the far side of which is a new National Trust sign for Cwm Cynwyn.

This stony track is popularly known as the Roman Road (see A11).

3. Fifty metres on the left is a gate which leads into a walled enclosure at the end of which is a second gate. Follow through these and down the rough track to another gate and so to the farm (new Cwmcynwyn) via the lane to the right. Pass through the farmyard

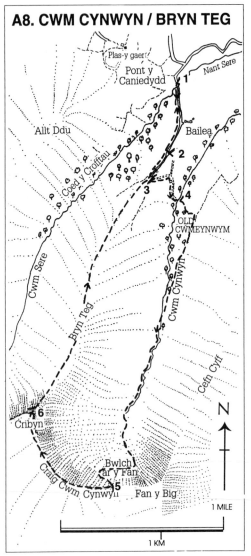

A8. CWM CYNWYN / BRYN TEG

to a gate and through this to a stony lane where ahead is a fine view of Fan y Big. At the bottom of this stony lane the track bears to the right up the valley. Ignore this and continue dropping down left alongside the green moss covered stone wall to the stream.

4. Cross the river aiming for the gate opposite. Keep left up the hill to the top and round to the right into the grounds of old Cwmcynwyn Farm.

The fireplace still has its oak lintel in place and a surprisingly large tree emerges half way up the front of the chimney breast. Its roots have penetrated through the stones and into the ground below.

From the ruins turn left by the wire fence and up the track to a stile and so to the path running along the hillside 50m above. Turn right (SSW), following the path towards the head of the valley. The hill fence turns right and drops down to the river bed.

In front of you on the right is the prow of Cribyn and the ridge running round from that to the gap of the Roman Road and Fan y Big on your left. To get good winter pictures in snow you must make an early start as the sun comes over the left-hand ridge. Later in the day the valley is back lit and mostly in shadow.

Continue along the east side of the valley above the stream down to the right. Eventually the indistinct path you are following meets the stream bed at a hawthorn tree and old stone enclosures (hafodydd). Leave the stream course here and strike up left onto the lower reaches of Fan y Big on which there is a double row of small rock outcrops which should be passed on the left-hand side. Traverse right above the lower outcrops and climb steadily to the Roman Road.

A8 Hafodydd in Cwm Cynwyn - The ruined stone enclosures in this area were originally small buildings and pens, called hafodydd, used when flocks were moved to higher pastures in the spring. One stone is inscribed with "GH", the initials of the Gwynne Halfords of Buckland, a large land-owning family in Victorian times.

You will want to catch your breath after this sustained climb and there are plenty of interesting features to see from this good viewpoint. Down below in the head of the valley is an interesting glacial feature (Head of Cwm Cynwyn). Up above to the west is the impressive crag of Craig Cwm Cynwyn (see A10) formed from resistant Brownstones (Geology of Brecon Beacons, see C1). Finally, you may well be resting on a once busy Roman thoroughfare (Roman Road, see A11).

A8 Head of Cwm Cynwyn - The hummocky terrain in the head of Cwm Cynywn is an interesting glacial feature. This was deposited by melting glaciers and consists of angular and rounded boulders in a sandy, clayey matrix which is known as boulder-clay. A marshy area below the headwall crags is where the corrie lake would once have been (see Route A1 Cwm Llwch/Cefn Cwm Llwch). Hare's tail

---

> grass *(Eriophorum vaginatum)*, soft rush *(Juncus effusus)* and
> sphagnum *(Sphagnum recurvum)* now thrive in the wet conditions.

Turn left at the Roman Road and make your way to Bwlch ar y Fan, the "gap between the peaks".

The gap is an ideal place to appreciate the almost perfect U-shape of this glacial valley (see A10).

5. From here climb west up Craig Cwm Cynwyn to the summit of Cribyn.

The lower part is the steepest pull but the slope becomes easier as you approach the summit.

6. From Cribyn descend steeply along the Bryn Teg ridge northwards down to the National Trust sign and so back down the road to the start.

The steeper section in the middle of the ridge is a secondary scarp formed by the transition from Brownstones to underlying Senni Beds (see C1).

A9. Cwm Cynwyn/Cefn Cyff

Start:	Pen-yr-heol
Grid Reference:	0577 2405
Distance:	8.75km (5.2 miles)
Height Gained:	410m (1350ft)

A fairly easy walk during which you can enjoy the beautiful valley of Cwm Cynwyn and the return via the ridge of Cefn Cyff. The valley has escaped being planted with alien coniferous forestry and deciduous woodland fills the lower reaches, giving a natural, timeless atmosphere. The valley provides easy walking but a degree of exertion is required for the final climb up to the "gap" and to Fan y Big. Interest is sustained by the plants and birds of the valley, the river scenery, the geological features and the views from Fan y Big, which are among the most impressive in the Beacons.

* * *

ROUTE

1. Start at the farm buildings just past the houses of Rhiwiau and

Glacial hanging valley from Blaen y Glyn from Craig Fan Las *(Routes B4 & B5)*
Fan y Big, Cribyn and Pen y Fan from Craig Cwareli *(Route A12)*

Early morning in Craig Cerrig-gleisiad after a light snowfall in later winter
(Route D1)

Sundew plants in Craig Cerrig-gleisiad *(Routes D1 & D4)*

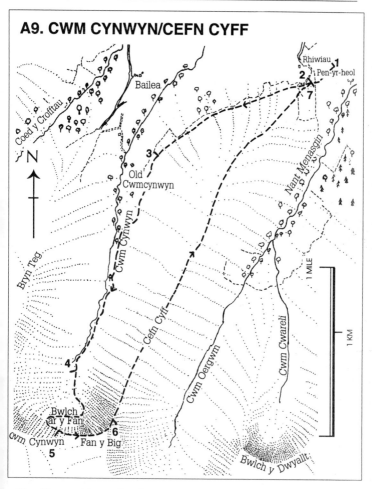

A9. CWM CYNWYN/CEFN CYFF

Llyn Fron at Pen-yr-heol.

From the sheep dip at the end of the tarmac road take a little time to enjoy the views east of Cwm Oergwm.

Do not go into the yard in front of the buildings but turn up the obvious stony track on the right (SW) to a gate which leads to the

open hillside.

2. Cross over the hill fence and follow the path which divides into two after a short distance. Take the main obvious track rising up the hillside to the left, avoiding the small track which appears to go down into Cwm Cynwyn on your right. The large track immediately divides again and the main track goes further up to the left. Ignore this and go straight ahead, contouring around the hill. The hill fence swings away down to the right, marked by a large birch tree on the corner.

Look back from here for a very good view of the Black Mountains stretching up to Hay on Wye. The track is well marked and obviously frequently walked and runs through bracken on the upslope side of the old hill wall and newer hill fence. Straight ahead you first see Pen y Fan with Cefn Cwm Llwch leading up to it.

The hill fence drops away to the right and continuing around the contour of the hill you cross a small stream and come to a group of hawthorn trees and a good view up to Cribyn on the left (up the ridge of Bryn Teg) and Pen y Fan to the right.

This point makes a fine photographic opportunity with the hills framed between the trees. Early morning light, as the sun comes over Cefn Cyff on your left, is best for photographs.

The view south-west to the head of the valley shows the ice-sculpted U-shape and the steep headwall (see A10). The notch in the col, called Bwlch ar y Fan, is where the Roman Road reaches its highest point before dropping into the Taf Fechan Valley (see A11).

Continue contouring across the slope and arrive at a stile over the hill fence on your right.

You can make a detour from the path over this stile to the derelict buildings of old Cwmcynwyn Farm as these are well worth a visit (see A8 Section 4).

3. From the ruins, retrace the path over the stile and turn to the right along the path above the hill fence. This path contours the hillside and into the stream bed.

Across the valley to the right is Bryn Teg ridge with its secondary scarp (Geology of Brecon Beacons, see C1) and the Roman Road running beneath it. This ridge leads up to the prow of Cribyn. Beyond it is Cefn Cwm Llwch ridge. Behind you to your left as you look up

Cwm Cynwyn Valley is the ridge of Cefn Cyff, the return route. Across the valley is the new farm of Cwmcynwyn.

The walk up the valley is most enjoyable. Hawthorn trees are dotted around on the grassy slopes of the upper valley with the level sheep tracks making a criss-cross pattern with the steep gullies created by water run-off. The head of the valley is formed by the steep slope of Fan y Big to the left and the higher crags of Cribyn to the right. The sharp nose of this peak is particularly impressive from this angle.

Scramble along the stream towards the head of the valley.

4. Leave the stream and strike up left onto the lower reaches of Fan y Big on which is a double row of small rock outcrops which should be passed on the left-hand side. Traverse right above the lower outcrops and climb steadily to the Roman Road and so on to the gap (Bwlch ar y Fan).

There are many features to be seen from this good viewpoint. Down in the head of this U-shaped valley is an interesting glacial feature (Head of Cwm Cynwyn, see A8; Glacial origins of U-shaped Valleys, see A10). Up above to the west is the impressive crag of Craig Cwm Cynwyn (see A10) formed from resistant Brownstones (Old Red Sandstone, see B3). Finally, you may well be resting on a once busy Roman thoroughfare (Roman Road, see A11).

5. Head east up the steep slope following the line of the crags to the summit of Fan y Big.

The summit has a block of sandstone protruding from its western side. An impressive photographic composition is made by someone standing on this with Cribyn and Pen y Fan behind.

6. Descend gradually NNE along the obvious ridge of Cefn Cyff which drops more steeply after 1.5km. The path becomes steeper again after another 1.2km of fairly flat ground, and drops north-east to a gate in the hill fence.

The step in the ridge is a result of the underlying rock formations and is a secondary scarp formed by the transition from Brownstones to underlying Senni Beds (see C1 & A10).

7. Pass through this and follow a stony track back to the start by the sheep dip and pens.

*Corn Du, Pen y Fan, and Cribyn from Fan y Big
with the Roman Road in the valley*

A10. Cwm Cynwyn Ridge Walk

Start:	Pen-yr-heol
Grid Reference:	0577 2405
Distance:	8km (5 miles)
Height Gained:	605m (1985ft)

A high level clockwise circuit of the ridges around Cwm Cynwyn. The route climbs steadily along Cefn Cyff and then more steeply to the summit of Fan y Big. A short descent is followed by a sustained climb to the impressive summit of Cribyn before one of the steepest descents in the Beacons to the ridge of Bryn Teg. All high ridges in the Beacons can be subject to rapid weather deterioration, and compass and map and the ability to use them are important. Two high peaks are included, demanding reasonable fitness. The glacial valleys and panoramas from the summits provide interest throughout the walk.

* * *

A10. CWM CYNWYN RIDGE WALK

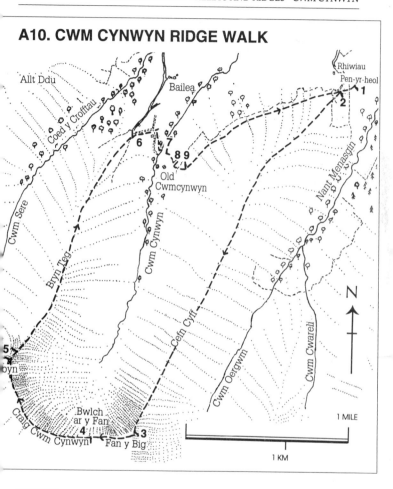

ROUTE

1. Start at the farm buildings beyond the houses of Rhiwiau and Llyn Fron at Pen-yr-heol. Do not go into the yard in front of the buildings but turn up the obvious stony track on the right (SW) to a gate which leads to the open hillside.

2. Head straight up the ridge ahead, eventually picking up a distinctive path marked by two cairns. Continue along the ridge to the summit of Fan y Big.

A10 Cefn Cyff - The ridge of Cefn Cyff forms a useful foreground for photographs. Interesting features include crags and peat ponds for pictures of Cribyn. Towards the northern end of Cefn Cyff, the view south-west is of the valleys and ridges leading up to the summits. The steeper section in the middle of the ridge is a secondary scarp formed by the transition from Brownstones to underlying Senni Beds (Geology of Brecon Beacons, see C1). The top of the ridge is covered in heavily grazed blanket mire which is mostly hare's tail grass *(Eriophorum vaginatum)* with some ling *(Calluna)*, deer grass *(Trichophorum cespitosum)* and bilberry *(Vaccinium myrtilius)*. The sides of the ridge are covered in heath rush/mat grass *(Juncus squarrosus/Nardus)* grassland which grades into mat grass on lower slopes and then into bracken.

The summit has a block of sandstone protruding from its western side. An impressive photographic composition is made by someone standing on this with Cribyn and Pen y Fan behind.

3. Descend west to the Gap (Bwlch ar y Fan).

Look below to the north for a good view of the head of Cwm Cynwyn (see A8).

4. From here climb west up Craig Cwm Cynwyn to the summit of Cribyn.

A10 Craig Cwm Cynwyn - The crags beneath Craig Cwm Cynwyn are accessible to grazing sheep and so are not as botanically interesting as the Pen y Fan and Cribyn headwalls, especially the highest ledges of the sheer north-east face of Pen y Fan. Vegetation consists mostly of mixed acidic grassland and purple moor grass *(Vaccinium)* heath on slopes and ledges between rock faces. The most inaccessible ledges are oases for herb-rich communities which include *Scabiosa columbaria*, mossy saxifrage *(Saxifraga hypnoides)*, viviparous fescue *(Festuca vivipara)*, brittle bladder fern *(Cystopteris fragilis)* and limestone bedstraw *(Galium sterneri)*.

The lower part is the steepest pull and the slope becomes easier as you approach the summit (Craig Cwm Cynwyn). From this ridge you have a superb view north of the perfect U-shaped valley of Cwm Cynwyn.

A10   Glacial origin of U-shaped valleys - The valleys were originally formed by streams cutting down through the Old Red Sandstone rocks forming a V-shaped cross-section. For some 2 million years this area was in the grip of the "Ice age" which ended about 10,000 years ago. Glacier ice carved out U-shaped valleys and towards the end of the Pleistocene, when climatic conditions were still sufficiently cold for significant quantities of snow to collect, many cwms were formed.

---

5.   From Cribyn descend steeply along the Bryn Teg ridge northwards towards a gate in the hill fence and a National Trust sign.

Notice the step half way along the ridge. It has the same origins as the step you ascended earlier on Cefn Cyff (Geology of Brecon Beacons, see C1).

6.   Fifty metres before this on the right is a gate which leads into a walled enclosure at the end of which is a second gate. Follow through these and down the rough track to another gate and so to the farm (new Cwmcynwyn) via the lane to the right. Pass through the farmyard to a gate and through this to a stony lane where ahead is a fine view of Fan y Big. At the bottom of this stony lane the track bears to the right up the valley. Ignore this and drop down left alongside the green moss covered stone wall to the stream.

7.   Cross the river aiming for the gate opposite and keeping left go up the hill to the top and round to the right into the grounds of old Cwmcynwyn Farm.

8.   From the ruins turn left by the wire fence and up the track to a stile and so to the path running along the hillside 50m above.

9.   Turn left along this and follow it above the hill fence to the point where you crossed it on the ascent. Continue down the lane back to the start.

A11. Cwm Cynwyn Valley Walk

Start:	Pont Caniedydd
Grid Reference:	0394 2439
Distance:	8.75km (5.6 miles)
Height Gained:	350m (1150ft)

A short valley walk in picturesque Cwm Cynwyn but be prepared to get wet feet! After crossing a small stream, the first half of the route follows the little explored eastern side of the valley. A short steep climb to the Gap (Bwlch ar y Fan) brings you to the Roman Road. This allows fast progress back to the start but do not forget to savour the wonderful atmosphere of this glacial valley as you tread in the footsteps of Roman soldiers. Route finding in a wide valley is always variable but safe and providing you can locate the "gap" in bad weather there are few difficulties. The main features of the walk are those described for Route A8.

* * *

ROUTE
From the start at Pont Caniedydd, follow Sections 1 to 4 of Route A8 along the eastern side of Cwm Cynwyn to the Gap.

5.   From the Gap head northwards back down the western side of Cwm Cynwyn to the hill fence. Follow the stony track, the Roman Road, and then the tarmac road back to the start.

A11 Roman Road - Whilst there is nothing specifically Roman about this road, it is extremely likely to be of Roman origin as the fortress at Y Gaer is near the mouth of this valley and the road would have been the natural link with other fortresses to the south at Pen y Darren, Gelligaer and Cardiff.

A11 Ancient landscape - The Brecon Beacons may appear to be a bleak and inhospitable place to live but prehistoric man is known to have settled here since Mesolithic times (Middle Stone Age c 6000 B.C.). The climate in Mesolithic, Neolithic (New Stone Age c 3000-1800 B.C.) and Bronze Age times (c 1800-400 B.C.) was much warmer and drier than today's and the mountains were covered in oak, birch, alder and lime woodland with an understorey of hazel and willow.

A11. CWM CYNWYN VALLEY WALK

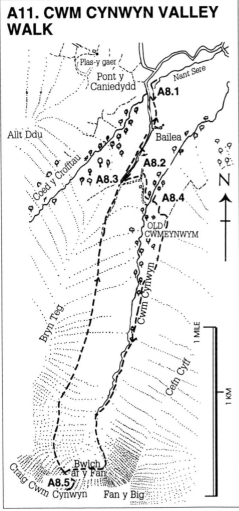

Woodland glades would have contained grasses, heathers, species of rose and various flowers. Prehistoric man fed, clothed and housed himself by hunting and gathering and, by about 2500 B.C., woodland clearance and mixed farming was practised. A marked increase in deforestation took place during pre-Roman Iron Age times in order to create new grasslands as sheep were an important part of the subsistence economy. Similar factors have controlled the appearance of the landscape from this time to the present day. The Upper Neuadd reservoir yielded many scrapers, arrowheads and knife blades during the very dry summer of 1976 when the water level was extremely low.

CWM OERGWM

A12. Cwm Oergwm/Cefn Cyff

Start: Pen-yr-heol
Grid Reference: 0577 2405
Distance: 9.75km (6 miles)
Height Gained   436m (1430ft)

The walk follows the western side of Cwm Oergwm through fields and some woodland to emerge onto open hillside at the hill fence. From here it drops to the stream below to a scenic waterfall and then up the stream course to the head of the valley. The headwall is climbed by a steep ascent to the lowest point of the ridge which is then followed north-west to Fan y Big. A long gentle descent along Cefn Cyff brings the walk to an end. Following the stream provides easy route finding and the ascent of the headwall is straightforward but steep and the alternative route ascending to Craig Cwareli is even more strenuous. The flowers and birdlife in the valley are extremely varied and complement the waterfall and mountain scenery.

* * *

ROUTE
1. Start at the farm buildings just past the houses of Rhiwiau and Llyn Fron. Leave the sheep pens on your right and follow the waymarked path into the field in front of the pens. In 100m it rejoins the track.

The deciduous woodland a little way down on the opposite side of the valley hides two Iron Age hill forts, Coed y Brenin and Coed y Caerau. The woodland occupying the valley floor is owned and managed by the Brecknock Wildlife Trust (see A13).

> **A12 Coed y Brenin Hill Fort** - The poorly preserved defences of this almost rectangular Iron Age hill fort are situated in Coed y Brenin overlooking the entrance to Cwm Oergwm. It is marked on the map as a "homestead". Natural protection is afforded by deep stream gullies on the east and west and the slope dropping away north-west but the fort is vulnerable to the south-east where the slope rises steeply.

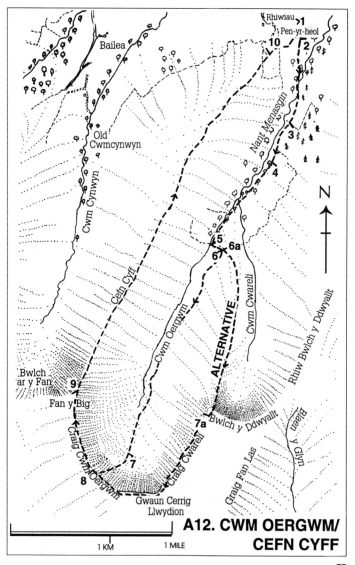

**A12. CWM OERGWM/
CEFN CYFF**

1 KM   1 MILE

A12 Coed y Caerau Hill Fort - Just to the east of the "homestead" is a "settlement". This is another Iron Age hill fort, again naturally protected by stream gullies on either side but overlooked by ground rising steeply to the south-west. The highest fortifications face uphill to defend this weakest point and are well preserved. Charcoal debris has been found inside the ramparts on a level, oval platform. Other platforms have been discovered in nearby woodland and these are ancient charcoal-burning hearths.

Continue for 200m and cross a stile. The route follows a clearly defined, slightly sunken track between mainly hawthorn, alder and ash.

2.   Coming to a gate there is a good view into Cwm Oergwm. From here follow the overgrown track between trees, with an old stone wall on the left, to a gate and a stream bed. Below, on the left, are the remains of buildings but the track continues and divides 200m further on near a metal store for sheep fodder.

3.   Leave this hut on your right and after twenty paces take the track down to the left and continue along the upper edge of deciduous forestry and into woodland. This part of the route is difficult to follow as there is no obvious path and care in route finding must be taken after the feed store is reached.

4.   Once in the woodland, head straight towards Cwm Cwareli to a gate in a stone wall. Beyond is open hillside and from here navigation is straightforward.

5.   Drop down left to the stream bed and proceed upstream to a waterfall.
   Once in the stream bed you will find secluded waterfalls and perhaps a heron hunting for fish. Buzzards are often found soaring on thermals overhead. Further on you come across a picturesque waterfall which makes an interesting photographic subject and ideal spot for a picnic.

** ALTERNATIVE ROUTE LEAVES FROM HERE **

6. From the main fall scramble upstream, encountering many smaller waterfalls on the way to the head of the valley.

Towards the head of the valley the stream has cut into mounds of glacial moraine left behind after the last Ice Age.

7. From the base of the headwall climb steeply to the lowest point of Craig Cwm Oergwm (GR 0377 1987).

This small col on the ridge is easily identified by piles of Brownstones and a number of dry-stone structures including a bothi built by the army. This is an unsightly affair as the roof is made of polythene and there is much discarded rubbish - the majority of which is easily identifiable as being of military origin.

8. From the col turn right (NNW) and gently climb along the eroded path to the summit of Fan y Big.

There are fine views as you walk to the summit of Fan y Big looking westwards to Cribyn and Pen y Fan. Fan y Big is easily identifiable by a distinctive sandstone block protruding on the north-west side. This block is well situated as a foreground feature for photographs of Cribyn and Pen y Fan.

9. Descend NNE along Cefn Cyff (see A10) along a distinct path to a prominent cairn made of Brownstones. Continue NNE along the ridge path which is now quite wide. Keep to the path along the top of the ridge to some old quarry spoils where a distinctive track to the left of these descends the end of the ridge. A good reference point to aim for is the church tower at Llanfrynach if you miss this track. The old quarry track winds its way downslope to a gate in the hill fence.

10. Pass through this and follow a stony track bordered on either side by stone walls with hazel, birch and holly back to the start.

** ALTERNATIVE ROUTE **
Follow Sections 1-5 above to the waterfall.

6a. Climb south-east to the spur which separates the side valley of Cwm Cwareli from Cwm Oergwm. The ridge high above is gained

by a steep strenuous ascent of this spur and might well require crampons and an ice axe in winter conditions.

7a. Turn right (SSW) along Craig Cwareli and around Craig Cwmoergwm to the col marked by piles of Brownstones.

The crags below have an interesting flora (see A14).

Route A12 is rejoined here at the beginning of Section 8.

A13. Cwm Oergwm/Gist Wen

Start:	Near Tregaer Farm
Grid Reference:	0715 2497
Distance:	13.75km (8.4 miles)
Height Gained:	540m (1818ft)

The route follows the eastern side of Cwm Oergwm through woods and fields to a waterfall. The valley bottom is followed to the headwall and a steep ascent is required to gain the col. The level ridge is followed around the eastern sides of Cwm Oergwm and Cwm Cwareli back to the start. Route finding is straightforward and the highest peaks are avoided so that only low mist would require recourse to the map. The walk is not over-strenuous but provides a great deal of interest ranging from wetland flora and birdlife to glacial scenery and two hill forts. The eastern ridge of Cwm Oergwm provides some of the finest panoramic views in the Beacons.

* * *

ROUTE

1. Start near the entrance to Tregaer Farm. Walk SSW along the road and after 150m another track on the right leads to Tregaer Farm. Ignore this track.

There is a fine view of Cwm Sere and Pen y Fan to the south-west from the gate here.

Continue along the tarmac road for a further 950m, passing Caerau Farm on the left. After another 50m there is a sign on the right side of the road which indicates a footpath 150yds ahead.

Directly opposite the modern bungalow (Cwm Oergwm Isaf) on the right is a stile with a right of way leading down to the stream. Up

A13. CWM OERGWM/GIST WEN

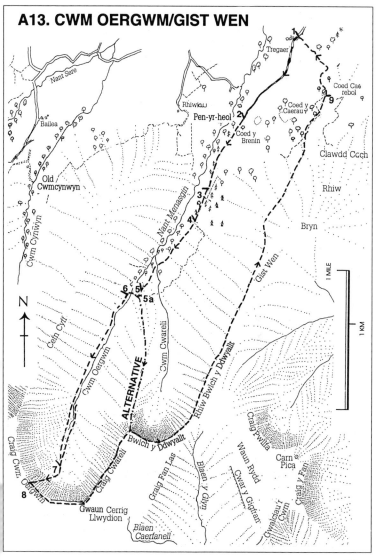

on the hillside to the south-east are two archaeological sites - a homestead and settlement. Unfortunately, there does not appear to be a public right of way to these (see A12).

The route continues along the road to a gate and the start of a bridle way.

2. Pass through the gate and follow the bridle way surfaced in coarse limestone chippings but which soon changes to a muddy track.

A forest reserve on the right is managed by the Brecknock Wildlife Trust. Look out for an old ruin at GR 0581 2282 that was probably once used for making charcoal. In this area you may see heron, raven, meadow pipit, skylark, buzzard, duck, finch and robin.

A13 Cwm Oergwm Woodland - The narrow strip of deciduous woodland found in Cwm Oergwm is similar in character to that found in Cwm Sere and is likewise managed by the Brecknock Wildlife Trust. The nature reserve comprises some 20 acres of deciduous woodland extending for almost a kilometre and a half along the steep eastern bank of Nant Menasgin. The valley bottom is wet and the species that grow here reflect these boggy conditions. Species found in these swampy conditions include trees such as alder and wetland plants such as great horsetail, kingcups and broad-leaved cotton-grass, the latter found in more open calcareous flushes. This reserve is also blessed with woodland birds typical of the north-eastern valleys. You may well see redstarts, pied flycatchers and buzzards.

---

3. A gate leads to dense coniferous forestry for 300m before passing through a second gate and into more open hillside.

4. Leave the sheep pens on the left and follow a marked path through land owned by the National Trust. After 1km the hill fence is reached.

5. Pass through a gate and turn right following a ditch alongside the fence to the stream below. Cross over using a few stones and follow the eastern bank to a waterfall.

Heron

Nant Menasgin tumbles over a number of small waterfalls created by more resistant bands of sandstone but is a "misfit" in this valley. This is because the classic U-shape was carved by glacier ice and not scoured away by the stream (see A10).

Look out for birds such as dippers and wagtails darting low over the water and, if you are very quiet, you may well be able to watch a heron stalking fish. Buzzards are often found soaring on thermals overhead. Further on you come across a picturesque waterfall which makes an interesting photographic subject and an ideal spot for a picnic.

** ALTERNATIVE ROUTE LEAVES FROM HERE **

6. Continue following the stream to the head of the valley.

Towards the head of the valley the stream has cut into mounds of glacial moraine left behind after the last Ice Age. The ruddy-brown crags high up to the left and right are formed by resistant bands of Brownstones (Geology of Brecon Beacons, see C1).

Brecon Beacons from Craig Cwm Oergwm

7. **Climb steeply to the right to the lowest point of Craig Cwm Oergwm (GR 0377 1987).**

This small col is easily identified by piles of Brownstones and a number of dry-stone structures including a bothi built by the army. Shelter can be found here for a well earned rest, snack and warm drink, especially if the weather is inclement.

8. **Turn left (SE) and follow the ridge path around the head of the valley to Craig Cwareli and on to Bwlch y Ddwyallt, Rhiw Bwlch y Ddwyallt and Gist Wen. Follow the obvious path, Ffordd Las or Bwlch Main, passing below the rounded summit of Bryn on your right. This part of the Route is about 5km.**

The disused sandstone quarries on Bryn were once worked for local building stone.

Continue along the well-worn path, descending Rhiw and Clawdd Coch, which then passes along the fence above Coed Tyle-du. Make sure you do not stray too far to the right and inadvertently reach the wrong gate in the hill fence. Once the fence above Coed Tyle-du drops to the left, make for the gate and stile in the hill fence just to the right of Coed Cae-rebol.

9.   Drop through the clearing, with denser woodland on the left and sparser woodland on the right, and then swing to the right to a gate in the corner of the field. Leave the farm of Tir Hir on the right and follow the track which swings down to the left along a line of trees, cross the ford and follow the farm lane back to the start.

** ALTERNATIVE ROUTE **

5a. Follow A13 Sections 1-4. Strike south from the hill fence and ascend the spur of land which separates the side valley of Cwm Cwareli from Cwm Oergwm.

This is an exciting and strenuous route and may well require crampons and ice axe in winter conditions. Below to the left is the glacial cirque of Cwm Cwareli. The disused stone pens are hafodydd or sheep pens (see A8). The steep inaccessible crags on the eastern side of the valley are an interesting arctic-alpine habitat (see A14).

6a. Join Route A12 at the start of Bwlch y Ddwyallt.

A14. Cwm Oergwm Ridge Walk

Start:	Near Tregaer Farm
Grid Reference:	0715 2497
Distance:	15km (9.3 miles)
Height Gained:	566m (1857ft)

This route follows the last two ridges of the north-eastern valleys. The ascent of Bryn is fairly easy from where you have one of the finest panoramic views in South Wales. After careful attention to the route in the early part of the valley, following the ridges is not difficult but be prepared and capable of using map and compass if the weather closes in on the higher sections. Height is gained and lost without undue exertion. The inclined geology of the Beacons can be appreciated fully from the eastern aspect and some of the finest views in the area are to be found.

* * *

ROUTE

1. **Start at a stile opposite the entrance to Tregaer Farm where a track leaves the road to the south-east. The stile is signed to Rhiw Bwlch y Ddwyallt. Follow this track south-east, climbing gently for a while, and then drop into a wooded gully and across a ford. Turn first to the left up the hillside along a track which soon bears to the right along the left side of the field following a line of trees and an old sunken track on the left.**

There is a good view over to the right of Pen y Fan, half hidden by the ridge of Cefn Cyff leading down from Fan y Big.

Half way up the hill there is a track off to the left to the farm. Ignore this and continue up the hill alongside the line of trees.

The Black Mountains can be seen well over to your left.

2. **At the apex of the field, with the buildings of Tir-hir Farm on your left, turn right to a gate and then left up the hill. The path winds through widely spaced small oak trees diagonally right up the slope to a more open area.**

Head straight up the hill, with the boundary of deciduous woodland of Coed Cae-rebol on your right, to the hill fence. This is crossed by a stile and the route joins a farm track rising from the left. The wall on the right swings further away to the right and the path steepens as it climbs the hillside to Clawdd Coch.

There are good views here of Pen y Fan, Cribyn and Fan y Big. The woodlands of Coed y Caerau and Coed y Brenin down to your right contain two Iron Age hill forts (see A12).

The path skirts to the right of the summit of Bryn, reaching a somewhat flatter section.

On the opposite side of the valley is Cefn Cyff which leads down from the summit of Fan y Big. Make a mental note here that this will be your descent route. The deciduous woodland in the valley floor is a woodland nature reserve (see A13). Due east from this point you can look down into the valley of Cwm Banw.

3. **From here climb for 2.2km along Ffordd Las which ascends first Gist Wen and then Rhiw Bwlch y Ddwyallt, meeting a junction of paths ascending from Carn Pica and Graig Fan Las. Continue round the spectacular ridge which swings around the head of Cwm**

A14. CWM OERGWM RIDGE WALK

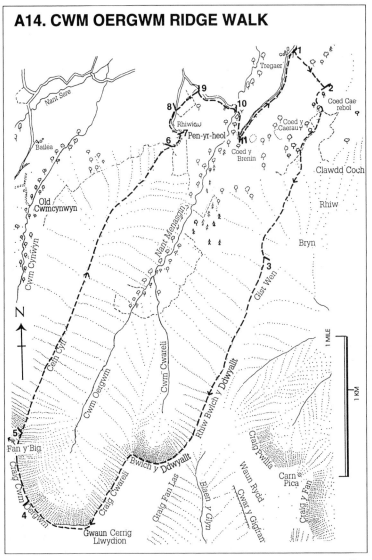

Cwareli and Cwm Oergwm.

The path is eroded and route finding is simple, but care must be taken in icy conditions or in strong winds as the route has precipitous drops immediately on the right. Craig Cwareli and the flat "lunar landscape" of Gwaun Cerrig Llwydion provide some of the best locations for photographs of the Beacons' highest summits. The dip slopes of the Plateau Beds which cap Corn Du and Pen y Fan clearly parallel each other from these viewpoints. The bedding of the underlying Brownstones exposed in the faces of Cribyn and Fan y Big are also in step. Seemingly endless photographic compositions can be found in this area, from wide-angle shots of all the peaks (using the lunar landscape as foreground) to telephoto shots of the summit of Cribyn, the dip slope of Fan y Big and part of the face of Pen y Fan. The crags below have an interesting flora.

A14 Flora of Craig Cwareli, Bwlch y Ddywallt and Craig Fan-las - Steep crags below the ridge path are inaccessible to grazing sheep in places and have some interesting species. Rock stonecrop *(Sedum forsteranum)*, mossy saxifrage *(Saxifraga hypnoides)*, purple saxifrage *(Saxifraga oppositifolia)*, and limestone bedstraw *(Galium sterneri)* have been recorded here.

Just around the head of Cwm Oergwm, the broad path drops into a small col, well marked by a military bothi.

4. **From the col, climb NNW to the summit of Fan y Big.**

From here there are magnificent views of Cribyn and Pen y Fan. The summit has a block of sandstone protruding from its western side and this is ideally placed for an impressive photographic composition of someone standing on this with Cribyn and Pen y Fan behind.

5. **Descend almost due north from the summit on an obvious path along Cefn Cyff (see A10) to old quarry spoils where you will meet and descend a quarry track to the left of these. The old quarry track winds its way downslope to a small copse and a gate and stile in the hill fence marked by a blue bridle way indicator.**

6. **Walk down the stony lane to a gate leading to Pen-yr-heol, the beginning of a tarmac road.**

7. Turn left past the white-washed cottage of Llwyn Fron on the right. Shortly the road swings down to the right with a lane leading to Rhiwiau Farm on the left.

Round the corner there are some coppiced beech trees about 50m further on the left-hand side. Coppicing is a traditional woodland practice which involves harvesting wood from a tree by cutting it down just above the ground, leaving just a stump from which new growth develops.

8. Take the first gate on the right, signposted with a yellow National Park Authority sign and a wooden sign to Llanfrynach. A path waymarked by two arrowed posts crosses the field to a stagger in the hedge. The right of way marked on the map follows the right side of the hedge but in fact the waymarked route passes through the gate keeping the hedge on the right.

Look back the way you have just come for one of the last views you will have of the summit of Pen y Fan. The field is improved grassland used to fatten ewes just after they have given birth in spring.

Follow the track curving to the right to a gate and a metalled road.

9. Turn right at the road, avoiding the temptation to cross it on the National Park waymarked route. Drop down the hill. As the road bears to the right, and on the apex of the bend before reaching the farm, there is a bridle way on the left marked by a sign depicting a horse and rider. Take the path (bordered by hedges of blackberry and wild rose) down to a stile and the river Nant Menasgin.

10. Cross over the stone river bridge, turn left then right up the waymarked track. Follow the conspicuous track which winds first left, then diagonally right, up the hillside.

The woodland here has an understorey of hazel with the odd oak, ash, holly, birch, beech, hawthorn and blackthorn.

The sunken path leads up on the edge of a field between two banks lined with mature trees. A stile is reached and a gate with a National Park Authority sign with a blue arrow indicating a bridle way up to the right.

11. Cross over the stile and turn left (NE) down the lane with a new bungalow on your right. Continue past the farm on your right and follow the tarmac lane back to the start near Tregaer Farm.

A15. Cwm Oergwm Valley Walk

Start:	Near Tregaer Farm
Grid Reference:	0715 2497
Distance:	5km (3.2 miles)
Height Gained:	200m (328ft)

A low level route in Cwm Oergwm taking the eastern side of the valley to a waterfall and returning along the western valley side. Once beyond the hill fence feel free to choose how you explore this delightfully quiet area with minimal exertion. The wildlife and the history of this valley provide more than enough interest. Since this is a valley, gradients are easy but route finding is slightly difficult through the fields and woods on the western side of this classic U-shaped glacial valley. This area is particularly interesting because of its woodland and bird nature reserve.

* * *

ROUTE
Follow Route A13 Sections 1-5 to the waterfall, GR 0497 2187.

6. Climb out of the stream bed, to the west, to a stone wall (the hill fence) with a stream gully running parallel to it and to a gate.

7. Pass through the gate and follow a path through woodland and then along the edge of deciduous forestry, eventually climbing diagonally to the left towards a metal feed store.

8. Leave this to your left and continue to a gate and a stream gully. Below to the right are the remains of old buildings. The path climbs gently from here, following an overgrown track lined by remnants of a dry-stone wall.

Pass through the gate at the top and follow a slightly sunken path to sheep pens beyond which is a metal road. The old path is

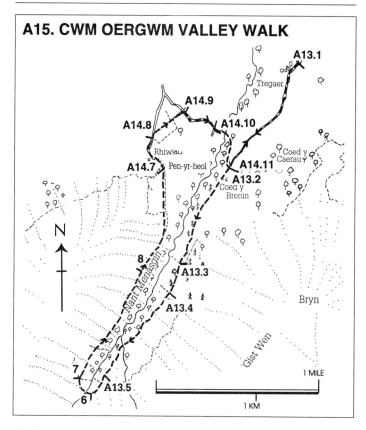

A15. CWM OERGWM VALLEY WALK

blocked by a gate some distance before the farm buildings but the route makes a detour into the field below, skirts below the sheep dip, passes through a gate and so to the metalled road.

On the right is a very old track which would be the quickest way but this is now overgrown and is no longer marked as a right of way.

Follow Cwm Oergwm Ridge walk A14 Sections 7-11 back to the start near Tregaer Farm.

Eastern Valleys and Ridges

B1. The Bryn

Start:	Pencelli Church
Grid Reference:	0874 2452
Distance:	6.25km (3.6 miles)
Height Gained:	386m (1266ft)

A varied walk with the initial stages passing through farm land followed by an excursion onto hill land to one of the best viewpoints in the Beacons. The circular route then winds its way through picturesque woodland with photogenic views of the River Usk (Afon Wysg) and the Black Mountains beyond. The beginning and end of the walk require care in path finding but height gained is moderate, making the route safe and fairly gentle. The main interest lies in the exceptional view from Pen y Bryn and in the solitude of the approaches.

✻ ✻ ✻

ROUTE

1. Start at the end of the tarmac road where it widens at Pencelli Church.

There is room for a number of cars to be parked here but do not take up space which may be needed by the congregation of the church.

Straight ahead is a tarmac track with the church on the right. On the left is a bridle way which is the end of the return route.

Take the track to the left of the church and after a few metres bear left off the tarmac track and onto a rough path.

The church is surrounded by yew trees, a species traditionally found in churchyards, and in early spring snowdrops can be found at the side of the church.

Pass in front of the house ahead, leaving it to your left, and follow a yellow National Park arrow which directs you down to the stream and over a wooden bridge.

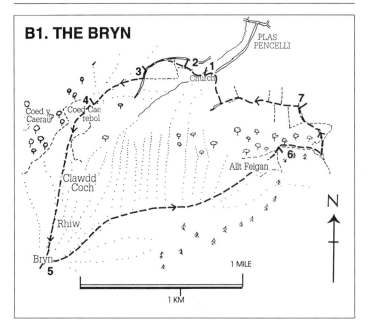

B1. THE BRYN

2. Follow the path up the slope and bear right through a gap in the line of trees ahead. Look for a gate in the hedge on the right and go through this, turning left onto the tarmac road and on up the hill.

At the crest of the hill take the track off to the right which is marked by a National Park sign.

3. Pass through the gate and along a track between hazel trees.
Look back for a superb view of the Black Mountains.
Cross over a stile and continue to conspicuous Scots pines.
Just past these is a good view of the north face of Pen y Fan (WSW).
Continue up the field on the right of the track and after 200m cut into the track on the left and over the stile at the side of the gate.

4. Once over the stile in the hill fence, keep close to the fence on the right. When this drops down to the right, head straight up left to the summit of Bryn.

Red grouse are thought to breed in this area.

B1 Pen y Bryn vista - The rounded, pool covered summit of Bryn (Bryn = hill, pen = head) is a superb vantage point for views and photographs, especially of the northern ridges and summits of the Brecon Beacons. Looking west, the first ridge is Cefn Cyff leading to Fan y Big, the middle ridge is Bryn Teg (fine ridge) leading to Cribyn and the final ridge is Cefn Cwm Llwch (Lake valley ridge). Good photographs of this classic Beacons scene are extremely difficult to obtain as an early morning sun is required for side lighting otherwise one is trying to shoot into the sun and hoping for some spectacular combination of cloud and lighting to make a dramatic composition. Even on clear mornings, the rising sun is blocked for a long time by the mountains to the south-west and during the shortest days of the year, when the sun tracks its lowest along the southern horizon, the northern valleys are barely lit. Looking north-west one can see Llyn Syfaddan (Llangorse Lake) and, beyond, the rolling wave-like front of the Black Mountains.

---

5.   At the summit turn north-east to a new cairn and head down left of the coniferous forestry with a bearing (060°) slightly to the right of Llangorse Lake which you see in the distance. Keep the coniferous forestry on the right and follow the track down the ridge. The track then cuts back to the left towards deciduous woodland, meeting this at a wall. Turn right along the wall and climb the stile into the wood.

6.   Once in the wood, follow the path down Allt Feigan. The path curves round to the right through oak and beech wood.

Follow the track along the left of the wall, which is now broken down, and on to a wooden gate and stile.

Ignore the path that leads straight ahead and swing left down the hill.

The wood is on the left and looking right over the fields there is a wonderful view of the River Usk meandering in the valley floor, with the Black Mountains beyond.

The track continues north-west along the northern edge of the wood to a gate and on to a second gate at the beginning of a wide track.

7. Turn left through the second gate and along the stony track but be careful not to miss this turn as it is easy to continue on down the hill. Follow the track and pass through the farmyard at Cornwall Farm. Stay on the bridleway, cross a small ford and turn right following the bridleway down the hill to the church.

B2. Cwm Tarthwynni Circuit

Start:	Talybont Reservoir Car Park
Grid Reference:	0996 1967
Distance:	7.5km (5 miles)
Height Gained:	570m (1850ft)

A fairly strenuous walk involving a continuous ascent of 480m (1500ft) over the first 2.5km. A short walk to a col is followed by an airy ascent up a narrow rib to the southern end of Craig y Fan. A panorama unfolds from this vantage point of the beautiful valley below and of the mountains to the east. A worthwhile extension to the route around Waun Rydd provides superb views of the summits, ridges and valleys of the Brecon Beacons. Most of the route is easy to follow but you may need to rely on compass bearings as the high plateau is reached. Expect to be challenged by the length of the walk and the stiff pull on some of the ascents. In addition to the quality of the views, you visit a Bronze Age funerary mound and see something of nineteenth-century intervention in reservoir and railway construction.

✳ ✳ ✳

ROUTE
1. Leave the car park, cross the road and go through a double gate with a sign "Forestry Commission Road - no admittance to vehicles". Go up this tarmac road for about 50m to a stile on the right. Leave the road here and follow a grassy track between two fences with the stream of Nant Tarthwynni down in the valley to the right.
   The old walls on either side of the track are lined with hazel. Straight up the valley you can see Carn Pica, the large cairn on the top of the summit.

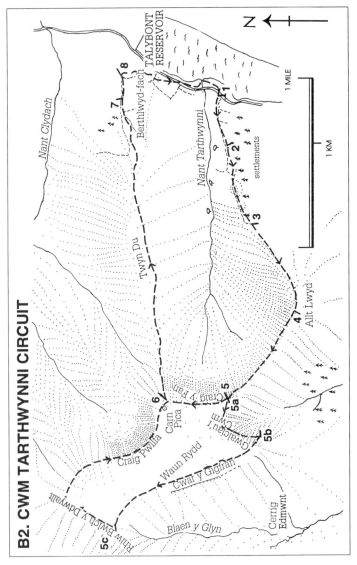

B2. CWM TARTHWYNNI CIRCUIT

TALYBONT RESERVOIR

Nant Clydach

Berthlwyd-fach

Nant Tarthwynni

settlements

Twyn Du

Allt Lwyd

Craig y Fan

Carn Pica

Craig Pwllfa

Gwalciau'r Cwm

Waun Rydd

Cwar y Gigfran

Rhiw Bwlch y Ddwyallt

Blaen y Glyn

Cerrig Edmwnt

1 MILE

1 KM

2. As you climb this grassy track, with rushes *(Juncus)* **on either side, you come to another gate and stile. Crossing over this you reach a steep field with stone walls on either side and the coniferous forestry plantation up to the left.**

The slopes of the valley are mainly covered in bracken with some deciduous woodland dotted around on the lower slopes.

Walk up this field keeping the wall on the right close to you until it drops steeply to the right. From this corner cut up across the slope to the end of the coniferous forestry where there is a gate in the far corner of the field (GR 0880 1941).

Walking up the valley you have a good view of the cliff at the end (Craig y Fan) with the stream running straight into its head. Looking back down the slope you can see the head of the Talybont Reservoir and beyond to the main ridges of the Black Mountains. Two settlements are marked on the Ordnance Survey map and these were once Iron Age hill forts which may have formed part of a settlement complex. The northern perimeters of both forts lie in the field you are crossing but the majority is in coniferous forestry plantation which has damaged and obscured most of this archaeological site. We wonder how this was allowed to happen!

B2 Talybont Reservoir - This is the largest reservoir in the Beacons and serves the Newport area. It was completed in 1938, flooding the valley and affecting 25 farms and 2875 acres of land, which was a compulsory purchase. Land around the reservoir was included and subsequently leased to the Forestry Commission. The creation of the reservoir made the surrounding hillside less viable for agriculture and the comparative fertility of the "bottom land" was reduced. Without it the higher rougher pasture cannot support stock. Forestry was favoured by the Water Authorities as it was thought not to be a pollution threat to water supplies in the same way as livestock. The area was created as a Local Nature reserve in 1975 in recognition of its ornithological importance and, in particular, as a wintering area for migrant birds. The reserve covers 490 acres and was set up by the National Park Authority through an agreement with the Welsh Water Authority and the Forestry Commission. It is managed by the Brecknock Naturalists Trust.

---

3. From the gate and stile in the hill fence, make straight to the summit of Allt Lwyd ahead of you (bearing 235°).

Just to the right is the col and the ridge which leads up to Craig y Fan.

Stop for a while on the summit of Allt Lwyd to enjoy the view. A rest will be appreciated before commencing the final climb. Vegetation on the rounded summit is dominated by hare's tail grass *(Eriophorum vaginatum)*, heath rush *(Juncus squarrosus)* and bilberry *(Vaccinium myrtillus)*. Localised patches of ling *(Calluna)* occur as well as common cotton-grass *(Eriophorum angustifolium)* and wavy hair grass *(Deschampsia flexuosa)*.

4. Cross north-west over to the col and ascend the steep prow to the top of the ridge, the last bit of ascent to gain the high Beacons plateau.

Surprisingly, the face to the right is at a much shallower angle than it appeared from the approach walk. It is made up of erosion resistant Brownstones which form the spectacular crags to the west and, if you look carefully in this direction, you can just see the two highest summits in South Wales, Pen y Fan and Corn Du (see C1).

** EXTENSION AROUND WAUN RYDD LEAVES FROM HERE **

5. Turn north following the head of this valley along Craig y Fan.

There is a good view down the valley with deciduous woodland at the bottom, Tor y Foel in the middle ground and the distinctive shape of the Sugar Loaf mountain in the distance. Look out for the interesting shapes created by the eroding peat hags on the plateau area of Waun Rydd (Peat Haggs, see B5). In colder months, icicles form on the overhanging turf and spectacular pictures can be taken by shooting through these into a setting sun. Waun Rydd is covered mainly in hare's tail grass *(Eriophorum vaginatum)* together with common cotton-grass *(Eriophorum angustifolium)*, heath rush *(Juncus squarrosus)* and scattered bilberry *(Vaccinium myrtillus)*, mat grass *(Nardus)* and crowberry *(Empetrum nigrum)*.

The top of the crag leads you to a distinctive landmark, Carn Pica, a large cairn made of sandstone.

Looking down Cwm Crew from Craig Gwaun Taf *(Routes C1 & C3)*
Entrance to Cwm Crew *(Route C3)*

B2 Carn Pica - Carn Pica is a modern cairn marking the site of a Bronze Age funerary mound. Pottery urns containing the remains of human cremations were placed in an excavated pit covered by large flat stones. A cairn was then built on the site. Radio-Carbon dating methods have given an early Bronze Age origin around 2200-1400 B.C. for these sites in the Beacons.

6. **From the cairn, descend the obvious eroded path E down a steep slope to the col and climb slightly to an area covered in bilberry with a little heather, Twyn Du, on the N side of the valley.**

Twyn Du has areas of hare's tail grass *(Eriophorum vaginatum)* and ling *(Calluna)* together with purple moor grass *(Molinia)*, crowberry *(Empetrum_nigrum)* and scattered cross-leaved heath *(Erica tetralix)*. Patches of bilberry *(Vaccinium myrtillus)* occur and this species is also found with ling.

Half way along this ridge you meet a rutted track - follow this down. This turns into a wide grassy track which drops down the side of the hill to the left (N) of the ridge and through a boggy area. Just to the left of this is the corner of the fence and an old dry-stone wall. Keeping the wall on your left, follow the grassy track down the hillside to a gate and a wooden stile. If you miss the track, head straight for the reservoir dam and the stile is easily found as the fences on either side funnel you to it. From here the path becomes obvious again.

7. **The path follows a gully carrying a stream on the right. Follow this downslope and, after a few hundred metres, cut across the stream to the right-hand bank. You are now on a raised bank with ditches on either side with a field on the right. Cross the small stream which joins from the right and continue to a gate on the right.**

8. **Through the gate and immediately on the left is a barn. Continue straight ahead for a hundred metres to a gate and on to some old stone buildings. Go between these with a stone wall on your left to a major track. Turn right here and proceed along towards a house called Berthlwyd-fach.**

Waterfall in Blaen-y-glyn

Cross over the cattle grid. The public right of way passes just above the house and is marked incorrectly on the definitive Ordnance Survey Map. Turn left after the cattle grid through a gate, head for the fence at the bottom of the garden. Walk across the slope to a stile in the hedge.

The route drops to the bottom left-hand corner of the field to a very old track lined with hazel and the odd oak tree. Pass through a gate and along a line of coppiced hazel trees parallel with the road. Go through another gate and along the track. In the next field drop to a gate where there is a stream and a series of old tank traps. Turn right at the road, cross over the bridge and walk a short distance back to the car park on the left.

** EXTENSION **

5a. Turn left (W) along the top of the crags around the head of Gwalciau'r Cwm to the end of Cwar y Gigfran.

From the southern end of Cwar y Gigfran the valley of Blaen-y-glyn and Blaen Caerfanell comes into full view. This is a glacial hanging valley with the stream plunging in a series of waterfalls into the valley below.

5b. Follow the top of the crags NNW and continue on this bearing, passing through eroding peat haggs (see B5) to Rhiw Bwlch y Ddwyallt, the ridge above Cwm Oergwm.

The inaccessible crags below provide an unusual plant habitat (see A14). The views from the ridge of Rhiw Bwlch y Ddwyallt are some of the finest in the Beacons and really capture the essence of the area. The valley immediately below is Cwm Cwareli. It has been deeply cut by the stream which later joins with Nant Menasgin in Cwm Oergwm.

5c. Turn right (NNE) along the obvious path and when it begins to drop contour around to the right (E). Gradually, the slope above Cwm Banw (the valley to the north) becomes steeper until it forms the steep slopes of Craig Pwllfa.

The glacial cirque below is the most sheltered area from the sun's rays in the whole valley and so was most susceptible to freeze-thaw action. The resulting moraine is called a nivation ridge that is now bisected by a stream (see D2).

Continue contouring the top of these to Carn Pica where you pick up the route once more at point 6.

B3. Blaen-y-glyn/Allt Forgan

Start:	Forestry Commission Car Park - Pont Blaen-y-glyn
Grid Reference:	0640 1690
Distance:	9.25km (6 miles)
Height Gained:	490m (1607ft)

This route combines the beautiful waterfall scenery of Blaen-y-glyn with a classic view of the Brecon Beacons' highest peaks. The walk gains height by following the course of the Caerfanell which plunges in a series of waterfalls. This now popular area is soon left behind as the route enters the glacial hanging valley of Cerrig Edmwnt. Finally, the ascent along the mountain stream of Blaen-y-glyn brings you to one of the finest vantage points in the whole of the Central Beacons. The return route follows the eastern valley ridge and drops to the satellite peak of Allt Forgan before the final descent back to the start. Route finding is simple as long as the river is followed but then take care as you climb up to the high ridges. A compass and map are needed along with the skills to use them. The walk is quite long and strenuous and the main points of interest are the waterfalls, the superb mountain views and the crashed bomber war memorial.

✳ ✳ ✳

ROUTE

1. Walk back to the main road, turn right down the hill and cross the bridge over the Caerfanell.

2. Cross over the stile on the left and follow the distinctive path north-west on the right-hand bank looking upstream.

This passes through mainly alder and hazel with some hawthorn, bramble and the odd birch. The river is the Caerfanell and its initial stages are quite wide as the water tumbles over a boulder-strewn bed. Keep glancing at the stream bed for a specialist bird of this habitat, the dipper. On a quiet day you are likely to chase a pair upstream for a

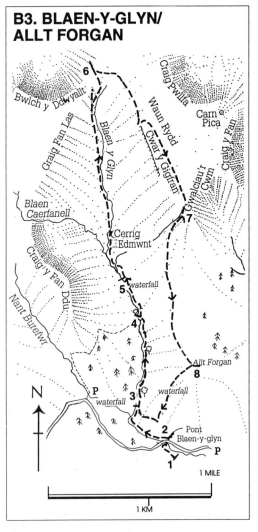

B3. BLAEN-Y-GLYN/ ALLT FORGAN

certain distance until they reach the end of their territory. At this point they will either hide or make a quick dash back downstream. Its companions, yellow and pied wagtails, are also abundant here. The reason for the woodland on your right being composed of alder is that the area is very wet and is fed by a number of springs issuing from the hillside above. Alder thrives in wet ground conditions and is characteristically found in boggy areas and along watercourses.

The best time to explore this area is early in the morning when the woodland is full of bird song. The riverbed soon changes character as the stream course narrows and you will come across a small waterfall which has a man-made rim and the water then tumbles over a natural exposure of Brownstones. At this point the damp alder wood is left behind and the slope up to the right is mainly covered in bracken with a prominent large oak tree. The banks of the stream are still lined with alder.

The stream is soon forced to run in a very narrow chute and just above this, beyond a right-hand bend in the stream, you will have your first glimpse of the largest fall in the lowest section of the valley. Just after the bend in the river you come across a confluence of streams.

The first of the waterfalls is encountered just after a wooden bridge crosses the stream. The fall can be explored by crossing the bridge and proceeding up the left bank. The valley is often in sunshine since it faces mainly south. This has the advantage of making photography relatively easy with the light coming from behind or to the side.

3. After exploring the fall rejoin the path which continues above the gorge on the right side of the stream.

Looking back down the river the high ground in front of you is Pant y Creigiau and below this is the line of the old railway cutting through the forestry.

B3 Old Railway - A continuous break in the forestry on the eastern side of the Talybont Valley is not a fire break but the course of the old Brecon and Merthyr Junction Railway. This was opened in January 1863 and tackled some very steep gradients, only to close a century later in 1962. The narrow gauge line (4ft 8.5ins) carried coal from Merthyr to Brecon and lime for agricultural purposes. This was made from limestone removed from extensive quarries between Pontsticill and Dowlais. The return trains hauled pitwood and other timber, cattle, sheep and pigs, cereals, beer and cider. The most difficult engineering task was the construction of a 666 yard tunnel at Torpantau through the ridge separating Glyn Collwn from Taf Fechan. Excavation began in March 1860 from both sides of the ridge with nine men in action, night and day, at each end of the tunnel bore. The final "break through" was achieved on 11 January 1862 and, amazingly, the two centres coincided within two inches.

Continue following the path along the stream valley which, after a short distance, straightens to give good views of the mountains ahead.

In front is the slope of Cerrig Edmwnt which leads up to the southern end of Cwar y Gigfran. On the right-hand side, in the near foreground, the valley sides are covered in oak and alder.

Continue up the path to the stile in the hill fence near to the stream.

There is an unusually large stone block immediately on your right above the hill fence which has been carefully inscribed with the initials G.H. and the date 1845. The initials may well be those of Gwynne Halfords of Buckland, a large landowning family in Victorian times (see also Route A8 where a similar stone is described on the wall of a sheep pen).

4. The path now works high above the stream which flows in a steep-sided wooded gorge.

At the end of the gorge is the last waterfall in this section. The path comes close to this and it is worth making a short detour to stand at the top of the fall and look back down the gorge.

5. From the fall the route keeps close to the stream passing a ruin where there is a good exposure of sandstone. Continue along the stream and follow the right fork (N) up towards the head of the valley. It is easier to climb up the left side of the stream gully where there appears to have once been a man-made cutting, possibly associated with the disused quarry.

The spoils of this can clearly be seen above to the right below the line of Cwar y Gigfran.

Finally, you join the main path and ridge of Rhiw Bwlch y Ddwyallt.

Your long climb is rewarded with a breathtaking view of the north-eastern valleys and ridges. The valley below is Cwm Cwareli which joins the classic U-shaped Cwm Oergwm. To the west (103°) are the three highest summits of the Beacons. Cribyn (height 795m) lies in front of Pen y Fan (height 886m) with Corn Du to the left, separated from the major summit by a small col. To the north is a green and yellow patchwork of fields and the town of Brecon (352°).

This scene is particularly dramatic if there has been a light snowfall as this picks out the relief in the steep faces of the mountains (Geology of Brecon Beacons, see C1). Blue skies, patchy cloud and an early morning sun provide perfect conditions for capturing an unforgettable scene on film.

6. Turn E and contour SSE along a path which winds its way through the peat haggs.

Continue to the war memorial just below the crest-line at GR 0620 2001. From here, climb to the end of the crags and walk SSE along Cwar y Gigfran to where it turns sharply north.

B3 War Memorial - This is a memorial to the crew of a Wellington bomber which served with 214 Squadron in 1941, taking part in raids on Hamburg and Rotterdam. Tragically, the plane crashed while undertaking a training exercise. It is likely that the mountain was covered in cloud with the pilot flying low trying to pinpoint his position. Each Armistice Day, wreaths of poppies are placed on the memorial which is close to the remains of the crashed aircraft itself.

The slopes below Cwar y Gigfran have a hummocky topography characteristic of landsliding. Here the rock and soil are slumping due to gravity, on curved slippage planes. This has resulted in backward tilting of upper bedding plane surfaces.

This furrow was once used for transporting stone from the quarry above and to the right. You will just be able to see the summits of Pen y Fan and Corn Du over the headwall of the valley to the west from the end of Cwar y Gigfran. Notice how well cleaved the Brownstones are in the cliffs here, making them break apart very easily to expose their bright red surfaces.

B3 Old Red Sandstone - Old Red Sandstone is a generic term which refers to a group of sedimentary rocks laid down by rivers flowing across coastal plains during the Devonian Epoch some 395-435 million years ago. Three distinct rock types, conglomerates, sands and muds, were formed from river gravels, sands and muds respectively.

The ridge is a fine vantage point affording views to the south of the hidden valley of Blaen-y-glyn and of the Talybont Valley and its reservoir (see B2). To the west are the limestone escarpments of Mynydd Llangynidr and Mynydd Llangattock. One can truly appreciate from this high point the scale of the decimation of this area by the coniferous forestry plantations. During the winter months the larch loses its greenery and it is then clear that it is often planted on the edges and as linear tracts within the forestry. The reason for this is that larch is less combustible and so acts as a firebreak.

7.   Descend the steep slope S to the col where you will notice a conspicuous furrow dropping straight down the slope. This was once used to transport stone down from the quarry. Head for a gate in the hill fence ahead where a dry-stone wall drops away from it. Keeping above the boggy area, go through the gate and strike up left to the summit of Allt Forgan.

This is a fine viewpoint for the ridges on the western side of the Talybont Valley. The vegetation here is largely purple moor grass *(Molinia)* together with ling *(Calluna)* and crowberry *(Vaccinium myrtillus)*. Again, you can appreciate from this viewpoint only too well the extent of the obliteration of this once naturally beautiful valley by coniferous forestry. Looking back up Blaen-y-glyn you have one of the best views of the glacial hanging valley. Look out for buzzards wheeling overhead.

B3 Hanging valley - The upper half of Blaen-y-glyn has been left "hanging" above the main Talybont Valley. During the Ice Age, Blaen-y-glyn would have contained a small glacier which fed the main glacier responsible for carving out the Talybont Valley (Glacial origins of U-shaped valleys, see A10). This glacier in turn fed one of the major glaciers of the Beacons which flowed down the Usk Valley. The stream which now drains the classically ice sculpted U-shaped hanging valley has cut a small "V" notch in the valley floor. The stream plunges over the "overhang" in a series of waterfalls.

---

8.   From the summit descend due west to pick up the line of the dry-stone wall. Cut down the zigzag path (W) to where a stream gully drops to the right. On a clear day you will be able to see some

stone ruins down to the right which is where you will pick up a track. If you cannot see these follow the gully downslope, keeping to the right-hand fork, and after passing the third large alder, turn left and pass above a group of silver birch. Continue diagonally downslope to some stone ruins and pick up a track here which leads back to the main waterfall. Retrace the path along the bank of the river to the road bridge. Turn right up the road and back to the Forestry Commission car park.

B4. Blaen-y-glyn/Craig y Fan Ddu

(Including a low level waterfall walk and a combination of the waterfall walk with a high level circuit of Blaen-y-glyn)

Start:	Forestry Commission Car Park
	(Pont Blaen-y-glyn)
Grid Reference:	0640 1690
Distance:	10km (6 miles)
Height Gained	490m (1608ft)

This route is similar in character to Route B3 but returns along the western side of Blaen-y-glyn and then follows another stream with a spectacular waterfall hidden in dense coniferous forestry. Numerous alternatives can be followed bringing great variety to the length and character of the walks. This is a part of the Brecon Beacons which can satisfy all interests and abilities. The route can be followed easily along the river bed but ability to read a map is needed in the higher reaches. The whole walk is moderately strenuous but this is rewarded by the waterfalls, some of the finest views in the Central Beacons and spectacular glacial features.

* * *

ROUTE
The first part is the same as for B3 Sections 1 to 5. Follow the stream past the waterfalls and all the way up the valley to the ridge of Rhiw Bwlch y Ddwyallt and the junction of four paths at GR 0575 2060.

** EXTENSION LEAVES FROM HERE **
6.   Turn left (SSW bearing 200°) and follow the path along the edge

B4. BLAEN-Y-GLYN/CRAIG Y FAN DDU

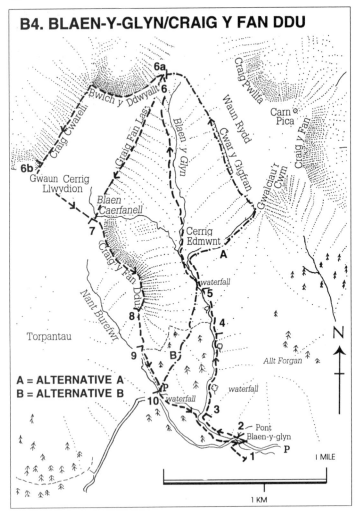

of Graig Fan Las and cross the stream of Blaen Caerfanell at GR 0504 1920 where it disappears over the cliff edge to fall to the valley below.

Looking back along Craig Fan Las the peat haggs of Waun Rydd take on a surreal appearance in the low afternoon light. The area to the right is Gwaun Cerrig Llwydion, also composed of eroding peat haggs (see B5). From this ridge the Mumbles Lighthouse can be seen on a clear day to the south-west, the sea sometimes glowing a deep red in a setting winter sun. Carefully inspect the exposed surfaces of Brownstone blocks (see B3) for evidence of ripple marks. Particularly good examples can be found on rock surfaces where the path crosses the stream which then tumbles over cliffs to the valley below. These ripples were formed in the beds of streams during the Devonian period of Geological Time (see C1).

B4 Gwaun Cerrig Llwydion - The flat lunar-like landscape of Gwaun Cerrig Llwydion and the ridge of Craig Cwareli provide some of the best locations for photographs of the Beacon's highest summits. From these viewpoints, the dip slopes of the Plateau Beds (which cap Corn Du and Pen y Fan) and the bedding of the underlying Brownstones (exposed in the faces of Fan y Big, Cribyn and Fan y Big) align (Geology of Brecon Beacons, see C1). Peat hags interspersed with areas of frost shattered Brownstones provide plenty of foreground interest and this horizontal plateau helps to balance the tilt of the Beacons ridges (Peat haggs, see B5). These rock fragments were produced by freezing and thawing at the end of the last Ice Age and have recently been exposed by erosion of the peat cover which developed in post-glacial times on poorly drained, flattish areas. This area is covered in badly eroding blanket mire which results in islands of peat being stranded amongst peaty channels or stone. Their tops are covered in hare's tail grass and common cotton-grass *(E. angustifolium)* together with occurrences of bilberry, heath rush *(Juncus squarrosus)*, wavy hair grass *(Deschampsia flexuosa)* and deer grass *(Trichophorum cespitosum)*.

---

7. Keep to the edge which now turns SSE (bearing 152°) along Craig y Fan Ddu. The obvious path tends to cut across to the right but following the crag line is more interesting even though the path is not so obvious.

8. Descend the steep prow of the mountain (S) to the edge of the

Waterfall just after the hill fence in the hanging valley of Blaen-y-glyn

forestry (GR 0545 1793).

The path is wide here and has suffered from erosion. The exposed soil can be very slippery in wet conditions.

> **B4   Blaen-y-glyn Coniferous Forestry** - Dense coniferous woodland growing in the Blaen-y-glyn valley is managed by the Forestry Commission. The plantation here dates from the late 1950s and originally consisted of Norway Spruce. Much of this has now been replaced by Sitka spruce, and Japanese larch *(Larix leptolepis)* is now planted instead of Larch *(Larix europaeo)*. The whole of the Talybont Valley has been heavily planted, shattering the ambience of a wild, natural mountain environment.

9.   From the corner of the forestry, continue on the path which now follows the stream-way of Nant Bwrefwr to the entrance of a Forestry Commission car park.

The steep banks of the small stream gorge are covered mainly in hazel, ash, alder and birch. Be careful not to miss a number of surprisingly high waterfalls to your right.

10. Do not cross the cattle grid into the car park (Talybont - Torpantau) but keep following the left bank of the stream, past three small waterfalls, and cross the river above the last of these. The path goes down the right side of the stream through dense larch woodland for about 100m to the top of a large fall. Cross back to the left bank above this and continue between conifers along a path. Eventually you are forced away from the bank of the stream but be careful not to miss the largest fall which has to be explored by dropping down a steep slope and then walking back up the river bed for a little way. Continue downstream along a path which follows the left bank and arrives at a track and a bridge along which you turn right and so back to the start.

** EXTENSION **
6a. From the ridge of Rhiw Bwlch y Ddwyallt at the head of Blaen-y-glyn follow the northern facing crag line around the head of Cwm Cwareli along Bwlch y Ddwyallt. Continue along Craig Cwareli until its direction changes to the west.

6b. Cut across Gwaun Cerrig Llwydion (bearing 128°) to where the Blaen Caerfanell stream cuts the southern end of Graig Fan Las and disappears over the cliff edge to fall to the valley below. Rejoin

Route B4, the main route, at the beginning of Section 7.

** ALTERNATIVE (A) **
Waterfall walk combined with a circuit of the head of the valley
Follow Sections 1 to 4 of Route B3 to the top of the waterfalls, where the gradient becomes more gentle and the forestry has been left behind. Leave the stream course near where a small tributary joins on the right and a wall meets the main stream on the left. Head north-east guided by a straight furrow in the hillside and climb to the southern end of Cwar y Gigfran.

This furrow was once used for transporting stone from the quarry above and to the right. The summits of Pen y Fan and Corn Du are just visible over the headwall of the valley to the west from the end of Cwar y Gigfran. Notice how well cleaved the Brownstones (see B3) are in the cliffs here, making them break apart very easily to expose their red surfaces.

Follow the crag line (NW) to rejoin Route B4 at the beginning of Section 6.

**ALTERNATIVE ** (B)
Low level waterfall walk
Follow Sections 1 to 4 of Route B3 to the top of the waterfalls. Cross the stream just above the last fall and walk south to a gate in the hill fence around the coniferous forestry plantation. This is being logged and replanted, so the forest roads are continuously changing in character. It is possible to find your way to the Forestry Commission car park where you join Route B4 at the beginning of Section 10.

** ALTERNATIVE STARTING POINT **
Torpantau Forestry Commission Car Park GR 0564 1755
The Forestry Commission car park at Torpantau is an alternative starting point for the upper parts of routes B3 and B4. It is useful for those not wishing to include the waterfalls in their route, making for shorter walks, but still with the opportunity of reaching the high Beacons' plateau. This is the highest road pass in the Brecon Beacons and is a good starting point for quick ascents to the high ridges.

The upper parts of Routes B3 and B4 can be followed by joining

Waterfall in the lower reaches of Nant Bwrefwr (see p109)

them at the beginning of Section 5 in the upper half of the valley. This can be reached from the Torpantau car park by continuing along the forestry track in a NNE direction. Turn left up a forestry ride and then right at a T-junction, finally coming across a stile in the hill fence (GR 0594 1816). Cross over the stile and strike NNE across the hillside to meet the stream above the last area of deciduous woodland and the last waterfall. This is where Section 5 of Routes B3 and B4 begins.

You now have the option of following the stream to the head of the valley and following Route B4 (Sections 5 to 10) back to the Forestry Commission car park.

Or you can follow ALTERNATIVE (A) up Cerrig Edmwnt and along Cwar y Gigfran to the ridge of Rhiw Bwlch y Ddwyallt meeting Route B4 at the beginning of Section 6. The latter option is a classic "horseshoe" walk.

B5. Torpantau Circuit

Start:	Torpantau Forestry Commission car park
Grid Reference:	0564 1755
Distance:	13km (8.5 miles)
Height Gained:	354m (1160ft)

An initial short steep climb to Craig y Fan Ddu is all that is needed to reach the high Beacons' plateau and a spectacular upland walk. The route follows the ridge around the head of Blaen-y-glyn and then around another ridge which forms the head of Cwm Oergwm. From the summit of Fan y Big, the route drops to the gap and a circuit of Torpantau brings you back to the start. The initial ascent is strenuous but once the ridge is gained the day's hard work is complete. Even in difficult visibility, the route can be followed easily by keeping to the ridges but compass bearings may be needed at the highest point. The geomorphology of the Beacons can best be seen from this walk and the viewpoints are spectacular.

* * *

ROUTE
1. **Walk out of the car park, recrossing the cattle grid, and climb immediately right up the path on the right-hand bank of Nant Bwrefwr stream with the coniferous forestry plantation on the right.**

Numerous plant-rich flushes can be found along the banks of Nant Bwrefwr. Interesting species include bog pimpernel (*Anagallis*

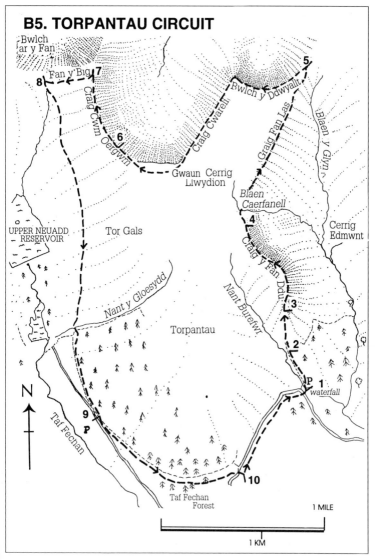

B5. TORPANTAU CIRCUIT

Bwlch
ar y Fan

Fan y Big **7**

8

Craig Cwm Oergwn

6

5

Bwlch y Ddwyallt

Craig Cwareli

Blaen y Glyn

Gwaun Cerrig
Llwydion

Craig Fan Las

Blaen
Caerfanell

4

Cerrig
Edmwnt

UPPER NEUADD
RESERVOIR

Tor Gals

Craig y Fan Ddu

3

Nant y Gloesydd

Nant Buretwr

Torpantau

2

P **1**
waterfall

N

9
P

Taf Fechan

10

Taf Fechan
Forest

1 MILE

1 KM

tenella), lesser valerian *(Valeriana dioica)* and marsh arrow-grass *(Triglochin palustris).*

2. At the corner of the forestry the path leaves the stream and heads directly up the wide eroded path for the southern end of Craig y Fan Ddu.

From this viewpoint you can fully appreciate the decimation of the Talybont Valley by conifer plantations (see B4).

B5 Coniferous Forestry - Conifers that are planted tightly together on hillsides throughout the National Park are alien to this area, having been imported for commercial reasons. They have been planted closely together to produce what is called a "close canopy" so that they produce straight stems with a minimum of branching. This technique has a disastrous effect on wildlife in that it entirely suppresses both growth on the forest floor and also any natural regeneration. There is a total absence of ground-flora, partly due to the intense shade and partly due to the carpet of conifer needle-leaves which produce an acidic surface layer. The humic acid produced from the breakdown of the needles contaminates streams and lakes and, if the receiving waters cannot "buffer" this acidic solution, fish and other life will die, resulting in a sterile environment. The trees are all of the same age and are "clear-felled" at maturity, leaving the areas prone to soil erosion and leaching. The end result is an area whose top-soil is sterile, since no fertile leaf mould has been produced, or with no top-soil where this has been washed away after felling.

---

3. Keep to the eastern edge of Craig y Fan Ddu and follow the line of crags north to where the small stream of Blaen Caerfanell cuts the path and disappears over the cliff edge to fall to the valley below.

Look closely at the rock surfaces exposed in the stream bed and you will see very good examples of fossil ripple marks. The valley below to the right is an interesting example of a glacial hanging valley (see B3).

4. Cross the stream and continue along Graig Fan Las (NNE) to a junction of paths on Rhiw Bwlch y Ddwyallt.

There is an opportunity for a pleasing photographic composition looking south down the valley and along the ridge at the peat haggs on Waun Rydd. Notice the classic U-shape of the hanging valley (see A10).

B5 Peat Haggs - These islands of peat are all that remain of a once continuous cover which has been eroded by water-cut channels. Peat is formed in boggy conditions when dead plant material accumulates and the process began in this area around 6000 years ago and continued for about 4000 years. The present climate is drier and this may account for the absence of peat formation in this area today. Man has not contributed to this decay by peat cutting at this site, but grazing animals have had a detrimental effect. Peat erosion has been further accelerated by excessive drying due to the wind and the sun and by the action of rain, frost, ice and snow. The cusp-shaped margins of the peat haggs provide essential shelter from the elements for sheep. Eventually, this striking topographical feature will unfortunately disappear completely.

Eroding Peat Hags on Waun Rydd seen from Graig Fan Las

5. Turn left (SW) and follow the ridges of Bwlch Ddwyallt and Craig Cwareli to the col where there is a bothi.

6. Continue following the ridge path along Craig Cwm Oergwm to the summit of Fan y Big.

The path is eroded and route finding is simple, but care must be taken in icy conditions or in strong winds as the route has precipitous drops immediately on the right.

There are fine views as you walk to the summit of Fan y Big looking westwards to Cribyn and Pen y Fan. Fan y Big is easily identifiable by a distinctive sandstone block protruding on the north-west side. This block is well situated as a foreground feature for photographs of Cribyn and Pen y Fan. The steep scarp faces of these ridges and summits are formed from resistant Brownstones (Geology of Brecon Beacons, see C1).

7. Descend west to the Gap (Bwlch ar y Fan).

Down below in the head of this U-shaped valley is an interesting glacial feature (Head of Cwm Cynwyn, see A8; Glacial origin of U-shaped Valleys, see A10). Up above to the west is the impressive crag of Craig Cwm Cynwyn, see A10.

8. Turn left and take the Roman Road south across the slopes of Tor Glas. Do not turn right on the track descending to the lower reservoir but stay on the track which skirts the lower edge of the forestry on your left.

You may well be walking in the footsteps of Roman legionnaires (see A11).

9. When the track meets the road at GR 0350 1740 continue along the edge of the forestry on a Forestry Commission ride which contours around the base of Torpantau and eventually meets the Pontsticill to Talybont road.

You will see signs of the old railway line here which ran from Pontsticill to Talybont (see B3).

10. Walk north-east along the road back to the car park.

South-Western Valleys and Ridges

C1. Neuadd Horseshoe

Start:	Taf Fechan Forestry Commission Car Park
Grid Reference:	0364 1710
Distance:	12.5km (7.6 miles)
Height Gained:	650m (2132ft)

The most popular circular walk in the Beacons taking in the three highest peaks in South Wales - Cribyn, Pen y Fan and Corn Du. The route is reasonably strenuous and the time required to complete it deceptively long. Route finding, however, is straightforward. This is a classic walk worth doing on quieter days. The most difficult sections are the initial climb to the ridge and the ascents of the main peaks. Some walkers may find the descents steep and tiring. It is difficult to exaggerate the views from this walk and the varied geology of the area can be well appreciated.

* * *

ROUTE
1. **Head north along the road to the Lower Neuadd reservoir.**

2. **Enter the reservoir grounds through the main gate, where there is a Welsh Water sign, and cut down left to a metal bridge. Cross this and climb up to the reservoir dam, crossing this to a gate in the fence and so to the open hillside.**
    From the dam you have the first opportunity to make a mental note of the route ahead. Up to the left is the ridge which leads to Corn Du and Pen y Fan. The route then drops to the col and climbs steeply to the summit of Cribyn before dropping to another col and returning via the Roman Road (see A11). An extension climbs to Fan y Big and contours above Tor Glas before following a gully back down to the reservoir to complete the "horseshoe". The lower Neuadd reservoir has been drained for some time and rhododendrons have now taken

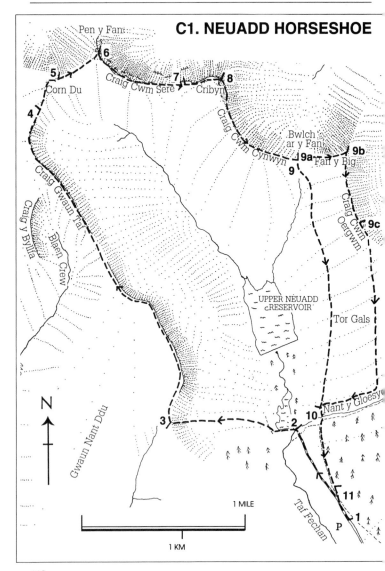

C1. NEUADD HORSESHOE

Pen y Fan

6

5

Corn Du

Craig Cwm Sere

7

8

Cribyn

4

Craig Cwm Cynwyn

Bwlch ar y Fan

9a

9

9b

Fan y Big

Craig Gwaun Taf

Craig y Bylia

Blaen Crew

Craig Cwm Oergwm

9c

UPPER NEUADD RESERVOIR

Tor Gals

N

Gwaun Nant Ddu

Nant y Gloesy

3

2

10

1 MILE

Taf Fechan

11

1

P

1 KM

Brecon Beacons from below Neuadd Reservoir

over the bed on the left-hand side.

Climb steeply left alongside the forestry fence and so up to the ridge above.

There is a good view during the ascent looking up the valley with Graig Fan Ddu to the left. Notice that the hillslope leading up to Graig Fan Ddu has a pronounced step. This is a well developed antiplanation terrace, a post-glacial feature (see A4).

C1 Graig Fan Ddu - The steep cliffs of Graig Fan Ddu have interesting crag plant communities including the southern-most occurrence of the dwarf willow *(Salix herbacea)* in Britain, its only locality in the Beacons. The crags have mostly ungrazed Vaccinium grass heath with a good population of sea campion *(Silene maritima)*. In general, the ledges are rather dry and less species-rich than those of Pen y Fan and Cribyn.

Once on the ridge there is a magnificent view west to the

119

Carmarthen Fan, to the Rhigos and the heads of the valleys. To the east is the Neuadd Valley, the headwaters of the Taf Fechan, that holds both upper and lower Neuadd reservoirs. South is the Taf Fechan reservoir. Back in the direction you have just walked is the distinctive shape of the Sugar Loaf near Abergavenny. North, through Bwlch ar y Fan where the Roman Road passes, you can see the Black Mountains.

3. Continue north along the ridge to a point above the northern tip of the upper Neuadd reservoir and from here you can see Corn Du, Pen y Fan, Cribyn and Fan y Big.

Across the valley can be seen the Roman Road coming up from the Neuadd reservoirs and crossing over the gap between Fan y Big and Cribyn and so on to Brecon. Looking left, south-west, down the Neath Valley on a clear day Mumbles Bay can be seen, as can the lighthouse on Mumbles Head and the smoke rising from the stacks of Baglan Bay.

The track continues along the crest of the ridge close to the steep drop on the right and care should be exercised in winter.

Towards its northern end the ridge falls off to the west and becomes the headwall to Cwm Crew. The rocks that make up the ridge you are walking on are called the Plateau Beds and these are well exposed in the northern crags of Cwm Crew. These have been eroded where the path drops to the col at Bwlch Duwynt (Windy Gap) but remnants are still left as distinctive flat caps to the summits of Corn Du and Pen y Pan.

4. At the end of the ridge descend to the col at Bwlch Duwynt where the track from the left comes up from Pont ar Daf. Ascending Corn Du brings you up the rock steps to the summit plateau. This is best crossed at its western edge and so to the summit cairn.

The rocky steps up to the flat topped summit of Corn Du are formed by a resistant cap of Plateau Beds. Corn Du is the best vantage point for views west of Fforest Fawr (see D5) and Bannau Sir Gaer, otherwise known as the Carmarthen Fan. Beyond the cairn is a superb view down the steep northern face into Cwm Llwch (see A2). The path which skirts below to the right of Corn Du can be taken if weather conditions deteriorate. This rejoins the route at the col before Pen y Fan.

5.   Now strike east, by a flattened cairn, and descend to the col and the well worn track up to the summit of Pen y Fan.

This col can be heavily corniced in winter and the walker should keep well back from the edge.

6.   From the summit cairn of Pen y Fan, leave at the southern end of the plateau on a well worn artificially stepped path. The path swings round to the east and drops steeply at first to the col.

Pen y Fan is the highest point in South Wales and, on a clear day, provides one of the finest vistas in Britain (Pen y Fan vista, see A4; Photographic Compositions, see A2; Ancient Landscape, see A11). As you descend Craig Cwm Sere, look to your left for a fine view of the north-east face of Pen y Fan (see A4 & A5). The National Trust, who own this land, have carried out extensive path restoration here. Keep to the made-up path to prevent further erosion problems.

The col is a natural place to stop and learn of the geological history of the northern Brecon Beacons (Earth Movements, see E3). Looking north down Cwm Sere you can see a perfect example of a glacial U-shaped valley (see A10).

C1   Geology of Brecon Beacons - The rocks forming the area belong to the Old Red Sandstone and were deposited some 395-345 million years ago in the period of geological time known as the Devonian. South Wales lay south of the equator in latitudes which are typically occupied by deserts. Prior to this, much of Britain was affected by strong earth movements which caused uplift and sharp folding resulting in a tract of upland, "St. George's Land", that

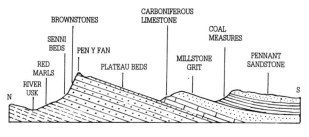

**Geological cross-section of the
Brecon Beacons**

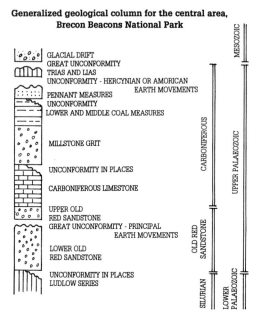

Generalized geological column for the central area, Brecon Beacons National Park

GLACIAL DRIFT
GREAT UNCONFORMITY
TRIAS AND LIAS
UNCONFORMITY - HERCYNIAN OR AMORICAN
                                    EARTH MOVEMENTS
PENNANT MEASURES
UNCONFORMITY
LOWER AND MIDDLE COAL MEASURES

MILLSTONE GRIT

UNCONFORMITY IN PLACES

CARBONIFEROUS LIMESTONE

UPPER OLD
RED SANDSTONE
GREAT UNCONFORMITY - PRINCIPAL
                        EARTH MOVEMENTS
LOWER OLD
RED SANDSTONE

UNCONFORMITY IN PLACES
LUDLOW SERIES

MESOZOIC

CARBONIFEROUS | UPPER PALAEOZOIC

OLD RED SANDSTONE

SILURIAN | LOWER PALAEOZOIC

probably extended from the Midlands through central and northern Wales and into Ireland. Flash floods washed down red muds, sands and grits along ephemeral river channels, building an extensive river flood plain. To the south was the Devonian shoreline, approximately where the Bristol Channel is now, and the warm Devonian Sea where the first fish were swimming. Europe at this time was drifting northward and, when it crossed the equator, the semi-arid flood plains were gradually submerged beneath tropical Carboniferous seas. The Old Red Sandstone in the Brecon Beacons can be split on geological grounds into Lower and Upper, the Middle being missing. The Lower Old Red Sandstone comprises a group of some 1500ft of red marls followed by a group of sandstones divided into two formations - the Senni Beds, some 1000ft of dark green chloritic layers interbedded with red, and the Brownstones, 1500ft of very dark red and purple sandstones. The steep craggy slopes are formed from these regularly bedded Brownstones. A secondary escarpment

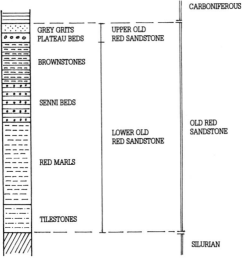

**Geological column showing units of the
Old Red Sandstone in the
Brecon Beacons**

CARBONIFEROUS

GREY GRITS
PLATEAU BEDS

UPPER OLD
RED SANDSTONE

BROWNSTONES

SENNI BEDS

OLD RED
SANDSTONE

LOWER OLD
RED SANDSTONE

RED MARLS

TILESTONES

SILURIAN

is well developed on the northern ridges of Cefn Cwm Llwch, Bryn Teg and Cefn Cyff where the ridge drops steeply from the main scarp and then flattens again between 540 and 600m and then drops again, the steeper slopes beneath this being cut in the Senni Beds which underlie the Brownstones. The Upper Old Red Sandstone comprises three groups of rocks. The Plateau Beds are red quartzites and conglomerates up to 100ft thick which unconformably overlie the Brownstones. The summits of Corn Du and Pen y Fan are capped by an isolated outlier of some 35ft of overlying, massively bedded, Plateau Beds. The second group, the Grey Grits, are unfossiliferous sandstones and conglomerates up to 200ft thick and these pass laterally eastwards into the Quartz Conglomerates which comprise red and brown sandstones, quartzites and coarse conglomerates. Further earth movements during the mid-Devonian uplifted South Wales resulting in renewed erosion, creating a distinct break in the geological record.

Craig Gwaun Taf from Corn Du

7. Ascend Cribyn steeply to another cairn.

8. Descend Cribyn following the path along Craig Cwm Cynwyn which swings first south and then east down to the gap and the Roman Road.

Stop at the gap and take in some of the interesting features in this area. To the north is the head of Cwm Cynwyn and up to the left is Craig Cwm Cynwyn (see A10). You may well be resting where Roman legionnaires once marched (Roman Road, see A11). Down below in the head of this U-shaped valley is an interesting glacial feature (Head of Cwm Cynwyn, see A8).

** ALTERNATIVE ROUTE STARTS FROM HERE **

9. Turn right (S) and follow the Roman Road across Tor Glas.

10. When you come to the stream gully at the southern end of the

lower Neuadd reservoir do not drop down the gully to the right but cross the gully and continue along the track along the edge of the forestry to the road.

11. Continue (S) down the road back to the start.

** ALTERNATIVE ROUTE **

9a. For those who still feel energetic, climb Fan y Big from the Roman Road.

Fan y Big is easily identifiable by a distinctive sandstone block protruding on the north-west side. An impressive photographic composition is made by someone standing on this with Cribyn and Pen y Fan behind. The steep scarp faces of these ridges and summits are formed from resistant Brownstones (Old Red Sandstone, see B3).

9b. From the summit, turn due south and follow the ridge path along Craig Cwm Oergwm to the military bothi at the low point of the ridge.

Below to the north is Cwm Oergwm, the last of the north-eastern glacial U-shaped valleys.

9c. Leave the main ridge path just past here and contour along the top of the slope of Tor Glas in a southerly direction. When you meet a stream gully (Nant y Gloesydd), just before the Forestry Commission plantation, descend following the right bank to the Roman Road at the beginning of Section 10 in the main route. Follow Sections 10 and 11 back to the start.

C2. Cwm Llysiog/Waun Wen

Start:	Pont Nant Gwinau
Grid Reference:	0077 1281
Distance:	8.75km (5.2 miles)
Height Gained:	220m (720ft)

A short walk based on Cwm Llysiog, a valley which has a bleak, isolated atmosphere, due to it probably being the least visited of all the valleys in the central Beacons. This feeling of solitude is really the only appeal of this walk as the access to the valley is via a monotonous climb through coniferous forestry with the return route crossing open moorland of little interest. The head of the valley has a number of picturesque waterfalls. No great height is reached so the walk is not strenuous but there are sections requiring very careful route finding in bad weather and the ability to take and follow compass bearings may be essential. The main features of interest are the waterfalls.

* * *

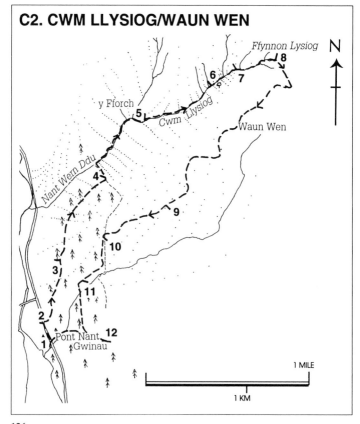

C2. CWM LLYSIOG/WAUN WEN

ROUTE

1. Walk north along the road taking care as traffic travels very fast here. After 50m a conspicuous forestry track leaves to the right.

2. Take this and climb up to the left through a mature Forestry Commission plantation.

A little way up on the left there is a very large beech tree and, a little further on around the edge of a clearing, some oak. The track continues to climb and is bordered mainly by larch, a deciduous conifer.

3. At a T-junction (marked on the map as a crossroads, the left turn is overgrown) continue straight ahead and after a short distance you come to clearings on both sides, the one to the left giving a clear view of the road and the river beyond, the Taf Fawr (Large Taf). Carry straight on, the forestry on the left becoming very dense and dark.

On the right of the track there are some interesting mounds of moss together with Juncus reeds and gorse.

This gravel-covered track terminates in a turning area, but carry straight on along an overgrown track covered in Juncus. Some 100m later cross the hill fence via a gate.

4. You emerge almost on top of the hillside, above the valley below on the left. There is a fine view directly into Nant Wern-ddu (Black alder bog stream).

Just along from the gate in the hill fence there is a good view of the lower reaches of Cwm Llysiog and the upper reaches of Nant Wern-ddu. A tree on the valley side provides foreground interest for a photograph.

Drop straight down to your left (NW) into the bottom of Nant Wern Ddu.

The lower reaches of the valley are totally blanketed with conifers but there are some deciduous trees lining the stream bed. Further up the valley there are a few scattered trees on the sides and adjacent to the stream. The river bed is wide and boulder strewn with a few diamond-shaped gravel bars. Reed-moss (*Juncus effusus-Sphagnum recurvum*) flushes are widespread along the stream.

In the valley bottom, near Y Fforch, there are some collapsed dry-stone buildings (possibly hafodydd, see A8) with a path marked on the map leading to them. The lower areas of the valley sides are covered in patchy bracken and above this is mat grass *(Nardus)* and heath rush *(Juncus squarrosus).*

5. Just after the derelict stone buildings, take the right fork of the river into Cwm Llysiog. Shortly, the sides become much steeper and it is easier to follow the left bank which is not quite so severe.

This area is quite attractive. The valley sides are dotted with birch and hawthorn with the stream tumbling over boulders and down a bedding plane for a few tens of metres. On the right are Old Red Sandstone exposures with red marls below. These are interbedded with thinner units of sandstone, with rowan growing out of them (Geology of Brecon Beacons, see C1).

Look out for flattened rushes and large amounts of rock debris brought down by small rivulets on either side of the stream, evidence of the Jeckyl and Hyde character of this valley. Notice the steamcourse runs perpendicular to the dip of the rocks and this is known as a strike stream. It is not a coincidence that the best rock exposures are found along the south-western bank as the erosive power of the water is concentrated in the down-dip direction, causing the stream to migrate sideways. Towards the upper reaches of this valley the stream bed narrows and twists between interlocking spurs.

C2 Flash Floods - Nant Wern-ddu has a reputation for producing flash floods and a number of measures have been taken in the past to combat this danger. A large stone embankment was constructed in the 1950s in the lower reaches of the valley in order to divert and slow down flood waters. A dam was also built half way up the valley at around the same time. The reason for this valley being prone to flash floods is that it is a "strike" valley since it lies at right-angles to the south-south-easterly dip of the rocks. You will notice from the map that there are more streams on its north-western bank (where the rocks dip towards it) than on the south-western sides where the rocks dip away from the stream. These tributaries drain an extensive upland area which rapidly supplies relatively large quantities of water to a small valley with a straight watercourse. These are ideal ingredients for flash floods.

NE face of Pen y Fan from Cefn-Cantref Farm
The final part of Craig Cwm Llwch from Corn Du *(Route A1)*

Sgwd yr Eira on the Afon Hepste *(Routes E2, E3 & E4)*
Pwll-y-rhyd where the Nedd plunges into the sink hole *(Route E5)*

Continue to an area of deciduous trees lining outcrops of Brownstones on the right of the stream (marked on map).

Just upstream is a small fall, about 3m high. The crags to the left are covered in ivy and numerous species of moss and ferns.

6. The valley splits again just after this fall. The smaller tributary on the left is well worth exploring with two small falls in a narrow gorge.

The banks are covered in heather *(Calluna)*, bilberry *(Vaccinium myrtillus)*, mosses, ferns and lichens.

Return to the confluence and follow the right-hand tributary to an impressive fall (3-4m high) with another a little further on.

Both are formed by thick beds of resistant sandstone, the first of Plateau Beds and the second of Grey Grits (Old Red Sandstone, see B3).

7. Climb up to the left of these.

From this vantage point there is a fine view looking back, the valley in the foreground having interlocking spurs with the larger valley beyond being more U-shaped.

A spring, Ffynnon Lysiog, flows from the base of Grey Grits along the banks of the last northern tributary which meets the main streamway between the last two falls. At this point the stream is covered in a film of orange iron hydroxide precipitated by bacteria. The waters issuing from the spring further up the tributary are rich in iron and have a reputation for their healing properties.

Just above the falls, the stream disseminates into flat open moorland, an expanse of bog with eroded peat haggs, dominated by purple moor grass *(Molinia)*, with hare's tail grass *(Eriphorum vaginatum)* and deer grass *(Trichophorum cespitosum)* in places.

The ridge along the southern side of the valley is the line of a geological fault which lies along the northern boundary of the Neath Disturbance. The rocks to the south have been down-thrown just enough to bring the Plateau Beds into direct contact with the Brownstones.

Up to the north is the flat area of Waun Lysiog and the slope above is Twyn Mwyalchod. To the north-east the line of coniferous forestry is part of the large Taf Fechan Forest, an extensive Forestry Commission plantation in the next valley.

8. From immediately above the waterfall walk SSE (bearing of 150°) across Twyn y Groes.

This is a wet area of purple moor grass *(Molinia)*.

Shortly (about 500m) you meet and turn right (SW) on to two parallel drainage ditches, about 10m apart and marked on the map as a track.

These meander south-westwards across Waun Wen, a large featureless area where there are patches of common cotton-grass *(Erica tetralix)* and heather *(Calluna)* amongst purple moor grass.

This open moor is quite a challenge from a route finding point of view and, with a covering of snow, navigation has to be done purely by compass as these ditches are lost from sight. The ditches become indistinct for short stretches but eventually appear to be double, parallel tracks, periodically marked by concrete fence posts, with barbed wire wrapped around them.

Gradually lose height crossing this moor and the coniferous forestry you walked through on the way up eventually becomes visible.

9. The route crosses a rivulet by a bridge of railway sleepers (quite a surprising find but perhaps a clue to some previous activity?). Straight ahead a gate leads into the coniferous forestry.

10. Pass through this and turn left after a short distance, along a wide forest track to Nant Gwinau. The track swings right, following the bank to a T-junction with a well used forestry track.

11. Turn left (south) and cross over the stream to the next clearing on the right marked by a dry-stone wall.

Across on the opposite side of the valley is Garwnant Forest Centre.

This junction is marked on the map as a crossroads but the track on the left is obscured when approaching from this direction and the track on the right is overgrown.

12. Turn right and follow the stone wall down the hillside to the

stream. Continue along the left bank down to the bridge and the lay-by.

C2 Birds of the mountains - Merlins have declined due to loss of open heather moorland which has been decimated by conifer planting, agricultural improvement of moorland and overstocking of sheep. Principal prey are meadow pipits which return to the moor in spring. Before this, merlins feed on small birds from surrounding lowlands, mainly chaffinches, tits and goldcrests. Ravens are numerous in the Brecon Beacons and are the great scavengers of the hills. Buzzards are also common and, together with ravens, are carrion feeders and find sheep carcasses whenever they can. Curlew can be found nesting among rushes of the higher streams but their camouflage is so good that you will rarely spot a sitting bird. Dunlin nest among eroding peat hags and are at their most southerly breeding limit in the world. Golden plover are another true wader of mountain moorland and are again close to their southerly limit. You may disturb red and black grouse when walking across open moorland, such as Waun Llysiog. Both species spend the winter on the mountains but the loss of bilberry, heather and cotton-grass moorland through conifer planting has resulted in their decline. Bracken covered valley slopes support dense populations of whinchat and also provide nesting areas for mallard, nightjar, stonechat, wren, tree pipit and yellowhammer. Damper patches may hide the dark-capped reed bunting. Skylarks are constant companions in spring and summer on grassy uplands, the air full of song as they fly above you. White rumped wheatear reside in dry-stone walls and bouldery scree. Look out for stonechat, linnets and yellowhammers amongst gorse.

C3. Cwm Crew/Cefn Crew

Start:	Corner of Forestry Commission plantation off A470
Grid Reference:	9925 1730
Distance:	7.5km (4.8 miles)
Height Gained:	420m (1500ft)

This is an interesting walk centred on Cwm Crew, a valley with an isolated feel even though it is adjacent to the busiest area of the Brecon Beacons National Park. Access is not easy and perhaps for this reason it is a very quiet and secluded area. From various vantage points during the walk a great deal of the surrounding countryside can be viewed and the route can easily be extended to take in Corn Du and Pen y Fan, the highest summits in South Wales. If the summits are included, the walk is quite demanding and, as in all mountainous areas, map and compass may be needed. The geological history of Cwm Crew is interesting and there are fine views from the top of the valley.

✳ ✳ ✳

ROUTE

The logical start for a walk in Cwm Crew would be to leave the road just to the left or right of the Nant Crew Bridge and follow the banks of the stream up the valley. There is room to park at GR 9939 1627, a lay-by at the north-east end of Cantref reservoir just north of the road bridge. Unfortunately, you have to cross 350m of private land to gain access to National Trust land and at the present time there is no permitted access.

It is worth stopping at Nant Crew Bridge for the fine view into the valley. A large oak stands guard over the entrance to Cwm Crew, providing the perfect foreground for a photograph. On a windless day the adjacent pool reflects the image of the tree but these conditions are few and far between as the prevailing winds are south-westerly and are funnelled up the valley. The depth of the pool is governed by the water level in Cantref reservoir and in a particularly dry year the pool disappears, leaving the gravel stream bed exposed.

From Nant Crew Bridge go north along the A470 to the start at GR 9925 1730.

1. Go through a gate in the hill fence and into National Trust land. Ascend the hillside on the north of the fence and over the brow of the hill. Drop down to the valley bottom, picking up a distinctive sheep track just above the stream.

2. Looking up the valley, keep to the left (NW) side passing numerous hawthorn trees. After a short distance, drop down past

C3. CWM CREW/ CEFN CREW

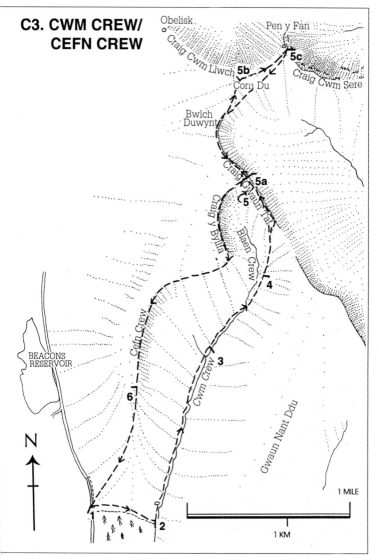

these and follow the river bed itself.

Interesting lighting conditions occur late in the afternoon when ribs in the valley sides are shadowed by backlighting.

3.   There are two sheep hafodydd (see A8) at GR 0037 1870. A path rises up above the river bed just after these, necessitating the crossing of numerous side valleys as they drop steeply to the river.

Continue past more stone hafodydd and just after these drop down to the stream bed to a small waterfall with a rowan tree. Keep in the river bed and examine small cliffs with unusual mosses and ferns on them. Below the next fall is a willow and the highest fall has to be bypassed on the right.

In high winds, the funnelling effect of the valley can cause the water to be blown vertically into the air in a large "spout".

Keep close to the river above the fall and aim for the end of a "tongue" of moraine which divides the streamcourse into two where the valley narrows before it changes direction to the north and becomes Blaen Crew.

The tributary to the right soon disappears in a boggy area.

4.   Climb up the prow of the moraine and continue diagonally up to the right to Rhiw yr Ysgyfarnog. Turn NNW along the ridge to Craig Gwaun Taf at the head of Cwm Crew.

From Rhiw yr Ysgyfarnog look back across the valley you have just ascended. Notice another moraine rib which runs down the slope from the southern end of Craig y Byllfa. Both this moraine and the lateral moraine you have just walked along were formed at the end of the last Ice Age when a lingering block of ice survived in the most shaded area of Cwm Crew. Rock debris from the steep slopes above the ice tobogganed down its slippery slope and accumulated around its edge.

The upland area around Cwm Crew together with a very narrow strip along Rhiw yr Ysgyfarnog, and the ridge south, still has its protective resistant cap of Plateau Beds (Geology of Brecon Beacons, see C1). Sandstone boulders on Craig Gwaun Taf (SW) are a good foreground for photographs of Cwm Crew. The cairn in the foreground lends distance to pictures of the Neuadd Valley.

From the ridge you have excellent views of the Beacons summits.

The peak on the left (due N) is Corn Du, followed by Pen y Fan, Cribyn and Fan y Big to the east. Blaen Crew very nearly became part of the Taf Fechan Valley during the Ice Age and all that separates them today is Rhiw yr Ysgyfarnog. The Taf Fechan (Little Taf) Valley below is the catchment area for the Neuadd reservoirs.

C3 Cwm Crew - This is a very secluded valley since difficult access dissuades most walkers. Unfortunately, it has not entirely escaped the alien intrusion of coniferous forestry on the slopes near the mouth of the valley. Once these are left behind, the valley has a truly wild feel with hawthorn and birch scattered around but in the upper reaches these disappear giving a barren appearance. For much of its length, Nant Crew is confined to a 15m wide straight channel within which it meanders. The dip of the rocks is to the south-south-east which has resulted in the northern and western valley sides eroding faster than the more stable southern and eastern sides where the rocks dip into the hillside. A few hafodydd are found on the valley floor, these derelict stone walled pens once used when sheep flocks were moved to higher ground in the summer. Upstream from these pens the stream changes character, becomes ever smaller and the watercourse is forced to twist its way around interlocking spurs of land. The stream bed now consists of exposed red sandstone bedrock

Glacial Activity in Cwm Crew

135

instead of boulders and gravel. Small waterfalls and pools are found where the confined stream tumbles over more resistant bands of Brownstone. Here you will find interesting rock exposures of micaceous red sandstone, particularly on the right (SE) bank. The valley changes character when it becomes narrower and swings around to the north. Cwm Crew is a classic U-shaped valley indicating that it was cut by a glacier. Much of the sides and floor are covered in unconsolidated sediments of glacial and periglacial origin. This "head" moved down slope over the permanently frozen subsoil during periglacial conditions which existed after the main Ice Age. The stream left in the valley then began to cut a sharp "V" down through these deposits resulting in the abrupt change of slope on either side of the stream. In places, the stream has washed away all these superficial deposits exposing Old Red Sandstone bedrock underneath. Waterfalls result when the stream encounters a more resistant band of sandstone.

** EXTENSION LEAVES HERE **

5. Turn west and follow the ridge of Craig y Byllfa which curves around to the south.

The crags of Craig y Byllfa are an impressive sight and are steep enough for snow to avalanche in winter. A detached block of Plateau Beds at the head of the valley is slowly creeping downhill, leaving a well developed landslip scar, the densely cleaved rock providing dramatic photographic compositions.

Keep to the high ground and follow the eastern side of Cefn Crew (SW) to where the ridge ends.

You are now overlooking the Taf Fawr Valley. Across the valley you can see the road to Ystradfellte running over the dam below the reservoir and up through the pine trees where it crosses a small road bridge. This is at a stream (Nant yr Eira) which is the start of the route up to Fan Fawr (Route D2). On the hill just to the right of the bridge can be seen evidence of an old homestead marked by concentric circles.

6. Lose height steadily by dropping down the prow of the mountain towards the forestry and make your way down to the gate in the hill

fence at the road.

** EXTENSION **

A worthwhile extension to the route is to visit the two highest summits in South Wales.

5a. Continue NNE along Craig Gwaun Taf and sweep around north to Bwlch Duwynt (windy gap) which certainly lives up to its name. Ahead of you is a well-worn path leading up to the flat-topped summit of Corn Du.

As you walk along the ridge to Corn Du you will notice that the Black Mountains are framed in the 'V' formed between Pen y Fan and Cribyn.

5b. From the summit descend east to the col and then climb gently to the top of Pen y Fan.

The resistant Plateau Beds which cap Corn Du (see A2) and Pen y Fan (see A4) have been eroded away on the intervening ridge which is composed of softer Brownstones (see B3). The ridge is eroding at a faster rate than the summits and this is a good example of differential erosion.

5c. Retrace your steps to the col but do not climb back up to Corn Du. Instead, follow the distinctive path which skirts along Corn Du back to Bwlch Duwynt. Follow the ridge back to the head of Blaen Crew and rejoin Route C3 at the beginning of Section 5 where you began your excursion to the high summits.

Fforest Fawr

D1. Craig Cerrig-gleisiad

Start:	Lay-by off A470
Grid Reference:	9717 2218
Distance:	3.3km (2 miles)
Height Gained:	280m (918ft)

A short walk packed full of interest. The route passes through the hollow of a periglacial cwm, overshadowed by steep craggy cliffs which are the habitat of rare alpine and arctic-alpine plants. This area is part of a National Nature Reserve and must be respected as such. There is a relatively short but steep ascent and the main features of interest are the glacial features of the crags and the wildlife, both plant and animal. There should be no difficulty in route finding but there is a steep descent that can be slippery.

* * *

ROUTE

1. Cross the stile to the right of the stream. Follow the path west into the cwm to a stone squeeze and a wooden gateway through the wall.

Stop and read the information board after crossing the stile as it explains the purpose and code of conduct for the area. There is now open access to the public. To the left of the stream is a laid out picnic area with trestle tables and a good view of the cwm. The stream and conifers just past the picnic site are useful foreground for photographs of the cwm but the crags themselves are rarely well lit. Just after the rising sun has cleared the highest Beacons ridges is the best time to visit.

2. Take the waymarked route into the cwm.

A pool in the cwm provides an opportunity for capturing a reflection of the crags (Geology of Brecon Beacons, see C1). An extremely wide-angle lens, less than 28mm, would be useful here.

Entrance to Craig Cerrig-gleisiad

There are botanically interesting boggy areas in the cwm which contain extraordinary species such as the carnivorous sundew *(Drosera rotundifolia)* which flowers between June and August.

Ascend the steep slope, along a path in a north-westerly direction, crossing a number of stiles, to a small cairn. Cross another stile and continue diagonally left across a bilberry covered slope to the top where there is a stile in a fence that runs north-south.

An ancient settlement site is marked on the map in the cwm.

3. Cross the fence and walk parallel to it, south, to a pool at GR 9595 2213. A short distance further on there are two stiles near a T-junction of fences.

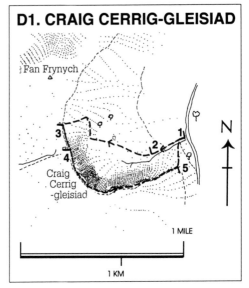

D1. CRAIG CERRIG-GLEISIAD

There is a Countryside Council for Wales information board just before this spot. The Council is responsible for management of the nature reserve.

D1 Craig Cerrig-gleisiad à Fan Frynych National Nature Reserve - The mountainous area of Craig Cerrig-gleisiad and Fan Frynych is of special botanical and geomorphological interest. It is owned and managed as a National Nature Reserve by the Countryside Council for Wales. Rare arctic-alpine plants are mainly found in the gullies of the steep crags where a cold, damp "micro-climate" exists and where they are protected from grazing animals. This special "micro" habitat allows them to exist at or near the southern limit of their range in Britain. Interesting species include purple saxifrage (Saxifraga oppositifolia), mossy saxifrage (Saxifraga hypnoides), green spleenwort (Asplenium viride), lesser meadow rue (Thalictrum minus) and northern bedstraw (Galium boreale). Moorland vegetation is made up largely of dwarf-shrub heathland comprising heather (Calluna vulgaris), bilberry (Vaccinium myrtillus), crowberry

(Empetrum nigrum) and associated grasses such as wavy hair-grass *(Deschampsia flexuosa)* and mat-grass *(Nardus stricta)*. Around 80 bird species can be found in the Reserve of which nearly 30 breed here. Skylark and meadow pipit are constant companions when walking over heathland with buzzard, kestrel, peregrine falcon and raven often sighted wheeling overhead. Look out for ring ouzel around gullies, wheatear on boulder-strewn slopes, whinchat among bracken and heather, redstart and tree pipit in hawthorn scrub, and dipper and wagtail darting along streams.

Conservation management - The area is owned and managed primarily to benefit nature conservation by the Countryside Council for Wales. Objectives are to re-establish a diverse dwarf-shrub heathland dominated by heather and bilberry and to encourage development of scattered hawthorn on mid-slopes and a more dense cover of trees and shrubs on lower slopes. These will be achieved by primarily controlling the numbers of grazing stock and by selective tree planting. Contact the Countryside Council of Wales for further information - Unit 13B, Mill Street Industrial Estate, Mill Street, Abergavenny NP7 5HE Tel 01873 857938.

4. Cross the stile on the right and continue along the path, keeping the fence on your left, following around the top of the crags. Take care when the path descends steeply east down a grassy slope.

5. Cut north through a hole in the wall at GR 9706 2195 and continue north, walking parallel to the fence.

6. Cross the stream and join the path again on the opposite side. Retrace your steps (E) to the start.

D1 Craig Cerrig-gleisiad - Craig Cerrig-gleisiad is part of a National Nature Reserve. The reason for this status is largely due to the rich plant life on the crags, including arctic-alpine plants, heather and bilberry heathland, and glacial features. A wide variety of birds breed in the area.

Origins - It is believed that the cwm was occupied by a small glacier during the Loch Lomond Stadial, the last period of glacial activity in the Brecon Beacons when small glaciers developed and perennial snow patches formed in the shadow of northern-facing scarps. Periglacial conditions existed beyond the glacier margins. This was the last cold period and it ended around 10,000 years ago. Persistent erosion at the base of the western wall by glacial and freeze-thaw action on the wall itself led to slumping and rockfalls. The hummocky terrain left in the hollow was produced by the last small glacier but some of it may have been left from the earlier Late Devensian ice-sheet that covered the entire Brecon Beacons around 20,000 years ago.

D2. Fan Fawr

Start:	Nant-yr-Eira Bridge
Grid Reference:	9880 1777
Distance:	9km (5.6 miles)
Height Gained:	350m (947ft)

This unusual route to the summit of Fan Fawr avoids the busier direct approach from Storey Arms. The walk gains height gradually by following the crest of the glacial cwm. A circuit of the summit gives fine views in all directions, including the Carmarthen Fan to the west and the Tarell Valley to the north. The route is best saved for reasonably clear weather because route finding can be difficult in poor visibility. No great exertion is required and there are good views across to the highest of the Beacons and down into a glacial cwm and moraine.

* * *

ROUTE
1. **From the bridge, climb up the left bank of the stream past a small waterfall and then above the stream bed where there are rowan trees. When the summit of Fan Fawr becomes visible the stream is crossed by some sandstone scars.**

Looking over to the north-east, the north-western ridge of Cefn Cwm Llwch rising up to Corn Du is visible and the valley below it to the west contains the head-waters of the River Taff (Blaen Taff Fawr). South of this is the ridge above Cwm Crew. Note this as it will be a useful direction marker in Section 5 of this route.

**2. Leave the stream at the sandstone outcrop and aim north for the
southern ridge of Fan Fawr (Cefn yr Henriw).**

From here look down into the cwm below the summit where the
moraine can be seen. This is called Cefn Bach. Looking back from the
direction where you started is the most northerly of the reservoirs -
the Beacons reservoir. The stream running down from Fan Fawr into
this reservoir is Nant Pennig. Looking to the north across the cwm is
the northern ridge of Fan Fawr which is the usual route up from
Storey Arms.

> **D2 Snow and Ice** - The route follows the edge of the glacial cwm
> which gives Fan Fawr its character. A most interesting feature lies
> in its base. This is a linear moraine marked on the map as Cefn Bach
> which runs parallel to the ridge. It could have formed when scree
> material from the back wall of the cwm slid down the surface of a

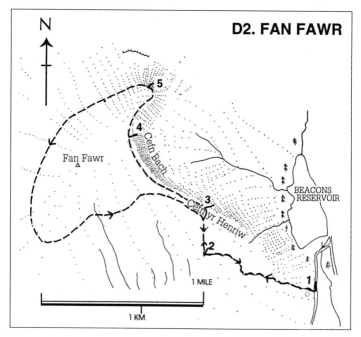

143

snow bed which had accumulated due to being sheltered from the sun's rays. This is called a nivation ridge or protalus. Another theory is that the moraine is of glacial origin and was formed when ice occupied the cwm.

3. **Follow the ridge along a sheep track and this continues up to the summit cairn which is to the north-east of where the trig point is to be seen.**

Note that the trig point is not sited at the highest point.

The view south-east from the summit of Fan Fawr includes the Taff Valley which contains the Beacons, Cantref and Llwyn-on reservoirs. The sides of the valley are covered with patches of dense coniferous forestry (see B5).

To the east, the summit of Corn Du lies on a bearing of 061° and obscures Pen y Fan which at 886m (2907ft) is the highest point in South Wales. The ugly scar of the footpath leading from Pont ar Daf to Corn Du is all too evident on a clear day. Due west is a superb view of Bannau Sir Gaer with the ridges of Fan Dringarth, Fan Nedd and Fan Gyhirych in the foreground. Looking due north is the buttress which hides Craig Cerrig-gleisiad (part of a National Nature Reserve, see D1) in the valley behind. Storey Arms, an outdoor education centre, is clearly visible on the Brecon road below Corn Du. The name comes from an inn which was lower down the road where the Pont ar Daf car park is today.

4. **Descend north from the summit cairn, following the top of the crags, until a steep slope is reached at GR 9725 1963. At this point you meet the path which comes up the hill from Storey Arms.**

5. **Follow the path which contours west around the north side of Fan Fawr or drop a little further down the slope and choose a contour just below the small rock outcrops.**

Look down onto the sheep folds or hafodydd below (see A8). On rounding the northern slope of Fan Fawr the receding lines of the Fans are revealed in all their splendour. Isolated sandstone boulders can be used as photographic foreground, their rugged texture contrasting with the subtle curves of the hills beyond. The western slopes of Fan Fawr fall away into Cwm Dringarth whose head holds

View west of Fforest Fawr from the northern slope of Fan Fawr

the Ystradfellte reservoir.

Eventually, you can follow a well marked sheep track round to the south-west where it starts to climb a little. At this point, strike up the hill in a southerly direction and contour round to the east side of Fan Fawr onto a level plateau south of the trig point. Aim for the southern end of Cefn Crew ridge, keeping well above areas of bog marked by rushes on your left. Keep above the spring line on the hillside.

The walk back across the open moorland crosses many rivulets and these later coalesce to form the Afon Hepste which joins with the Afon Mellte in the spectacular waterfall valleys of Ystradfellte (Section E).

This will bring you back on the ridge you climbed earlier. Retrace your steps by descending this and then walking to the stream in a south-easterly direction to the scars at the stream bed. Cross here and descend the right bank to the start.

D3. Craig Cwm-du/Fan Frynych

Start:	Near Forest Lodge Cottages
Grid Reference:	9617 2417
Distance:	7.5km (5 miles)
Height Gained:	270m (886ft)

A medium level walk with easy route finding in a relatively quiet part of the Park. An easy approach along Sarn Helen, a Roman Road, brings you to the entrance to Craig Cwm-du - a place of outstanding beauty that may remind you of a miniature Scottish glen. The area is of exceptional nature conservation interest, being part of a National Nature Reserve managed by the Countryside Council for Wales. An easy climb through heather and bilberry covered slopes brings you to the top of Fan Frynych for fine views of the Brecon Beacons. There are no great difficulties in following the route except on the climb to the summit of Fan Frynych. The area is quiet and unspoiled and presents a different character to other parts of the Beacons.

* * *

ROUTE

1. From the right-angle bend near Forest Lodge Cottages, take the stony track south-west to a gate just after which is a footpath sign "Coed Ty Mawr". Ignore this and carry on a short distance, through a second gate.

This straight track is Sarn Helen, a Roman Road. On your right is a small area of mixed deciduous and coniferous woodland and a pond.

Continue to a third gate where a track leaves to the left.

Make a mental note that this is your return route from the ridge up to your left where you can see a diagonal track leading down from the hill.

Pass through another gate and a few hundred metres beyond this on your right is a stile in the hill fence with a yellow arrow indicating a right of way down to Pontbren-garreg. Ignore this and continue to the next gate and cross the stile on its right.

The mountains ahead of you are the westerly "Fans" and in the very far distance you can see Bannau Sir Gaer. You are looking over Fforest Fawr (see D5).

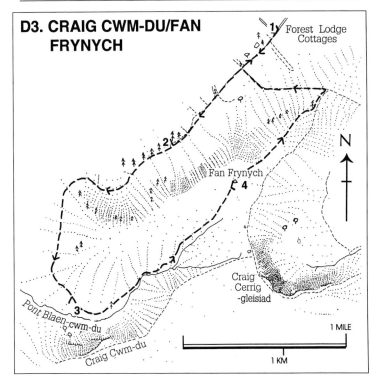

D3. CRAIG CWM-DU/FAN FRYNYCH

2. Here is a sign which indicates that you are entering Craig Cerrig-gleisiad, a Fan Frynych National Nature Reserve.

Unfortunately, the land immediately on your right is planted with alien conifers (see B5). The nature reserve is owned and managed by the Countryside Council for Wales. The warden can be contacted at Unit 13B, Mill Street Industrial Estate, Mill Street, Abergavenny NP7 5HE Tel 01873 857938.

The track divides after leaving the conifer plantation behind. The left fork passes through a gate and disappears over the skyline. Take the right fork continuing along Sarn Helen.

The left fork is an old drovers' road. Clumps of Scots pines were loosely planted on the bare hillside as an indication of the drovers'

147

route, to show where cattle and sheep might graze and where their drovers might obtain refreshment (see D4). As you round the next bend in the Roman Road there is a good view of the end of the Senni Valley with Fan Nedd to the left and Fan Gyhirych to the right.

There is a good view looking back to the north-east of Sarn Helen and the north-western slopes of Fan Frynych with copses of conifers.

D3 Sarn Helen - This Roman road linked Neath and Brecon and eventually with the coast road running from Chester to Segontium. It is named after Helen, Welsh wife of the Romano-British emperor Magnus Maximus. She was St. Helena, celebrated as the finder of the true cross and mother of the Emperor Constantine who was first declared emperor by the army in Britain. A fourteenth-century Welsh story in the "Mabinogion" tells how Macsen Wledig - the Roman usurper Magnus Maximus - dreamt of a girl whom he later discovered in Arfon and married. As a wedding gift she asked for three strongholds to be built at Caernarfon, Caerleon and Carmarthen, to be joined by roads known as roads of "Elen of the Hosts". A twelfth-century tradition, however, makes Helena the daughter of the founder of Colchester. The Romans had a hard struggle in controlling the Silures, a warlike Welsh tribe which ruled this mountainous part of South Wales prior to being conquered. In fact, from the time of the Roman invasion of Britain in A.D. 43, it took them around 25 years to subdue the Silures. The Romans ruled Britain for nearly 300 years and finally left, their empire in ruins, in A.D. 400. Sarn Helen continued to be an important road and was used by drovers taking their cattle and sheep to markets for many centuries.

Continue along Sarn Helen to where a track leaves to the left just before the bridge where there are ruins of an old toll house at the entrance to Cwm-du.

The pool at the entrance to Cwm-du would have been used by drovers to water their cattle.

3. Leave Sarn Helen by turning left up the track at the apex of the right-hand bend before the bridge.

The entrance to the cwm is a good spot for photographs and trees and sandstone boulders can be used as foreground for the crags. Lighting conditions tend to be difficult as the crags are invariably backlit except in the late afternoon.

D3 Craig Cwm-du - Craig Cwm-du is part of a National Nature Reserve having a total area of 493 hectares of heathland and crags (see D1). The southern valley side has been steepened by the action of ice forming 150m high crags on which grow a rich flora which includes arctic-alpine species.

Follow the track into the cwm to the fork in the stream. Take the left-hand branch. Towards the top, near the small waterfalls, is a sign indicating a left turn and a short climb. Follow this, working up left slightly away from the stream to avoid impassable waterfalls in the stream bed. The stream forks again and you take the left branch up a small side valley on its left flank. Follow this stream to a bed of cotton grass and reeds. Continue NNE arriving at Fan Frynych summit and meeting the track from Craig Cerrig-gleisiad coming up from the right.

Fan Frynych is a fine vantage point for views to the east of Corn Du and Pen y Fan.

4. From the trig point aim NNE, with the Brecon Beacons at about 2 o'clock, and pass close to small quarry spoils leaving them on your right. This stony track drops down to the hill fence and gate. The impression is gained of descending into the Tarell Valley but on reaching the larch trees and two gates and a stile, turn sharp left and follow the clear track down to Sarn Helen. Turn right to the start of the walk.

D4. Craig Cwm-du/Fan Dringarth/Fan Llia.

Start:	Sarn Helen
Grid Reference:	9250 1840
Distance:	16.25km (10.4 miles)
Height Gained:	212m (696ft)

A walk full of interest, both past and present. The Romans constructed

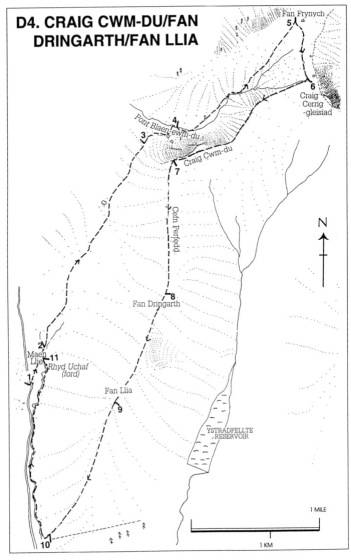

D4. CRAIG CWM-DU/FAN DRINGARTH/FAN LLIA

Fan Frynych

5

6

Craig Cerrig -gleisiad

Pont Blaen Cwm-du

4

3

Craig Cwm-du

7

N

Cefn Perfedd

Fan Dringarth

8

Maen Llia

11

Rhyd Uchaf (ford)

1

2

Fan Llia

9

YSTRADFELLTE RESERVOIR

1 MILE

10

1 KM

Sarn Helen road past Cwm-du, the Black Valley, which is now part of a National Nature Reserve. From the head of the cwm there are superb views of the rest of the Reserve, the crags and gullies of Craig Cerrig-gleisiad. Both of these cwms have an astonishing variety of birdlife, including buzzards and peregrine falcons. The return route crosses over Fan Dringarth and Fan Llia before dropping into the Llia Valley. The walk is quite relaxed and not too difficult to follow and it is in a rarely visited area of the National Park. If you enjoy seclusion, this is a walk well worth considering.

✳ ✳ ✳

ROUTE

1. At the point where Sarn Helen leaves the road, walk NNE up the stony track to the ford (Rhyd Uchaf).

Sarn Helen is a Roman Road (see D3). A few hundred metres further on, look left to see a large standing stone, Maen Llia (see D5).

2. After 2.5km pass through a gate to a Countryside Council for Wales sign at the entrance to Cwm-du.

Craig Cwm-du has the feel of a Scottish glen and any moment one expects to see a red deer moving among the Scots pines! It is the western half of a National Nature Reserve (Craig Cerrig-gleisiad à Fan Frynych National Nature Reserve, see D1).

The entrance to the cwm is a good spot for photographs. Trees and sandstone boulders can be used as foreground for the crags. Lighting conditions tend to be difficult as the crags are invariably backlit except in the late afternoon. The pool at the entrance to Cwm-du would have been used by drovers to water their cattle.

D4 Drovers - There are many old tracks in the Brecon Beacons which were used for many centuries by drovers. These men transported livestock from the agricultural areas to markets in England. Cattle were shod to protect their feet on long journeys and geese had their feet dipped in tar. The drovers returned from the markets with various goods for the farmers. Interestingly, they brought back gorse seed which was sown on the friddland, the steep hillside, often enclosed, up to 300m. Young gorse shoots are, apparently, a delicacy to sheep but they also provided shelter for seedlings such as thorn. A hard winter may well kill off old gorse but

---

the thorn seedlings may have grown just enough to survive grazing. A notable feature of the Brecon Beacons today are the dotted thorn trees on the valley sides which provide good nesting sites for merlins.

3. Continue to a stone bridge, Pont Blaen-cwm-du, where there are ruins of an old toll house.

The Roman Road swings away to the left here and ascends the hill.

4. A few metres further on take the track that leaves on the right and heads into the cwm to the fork in the stream. Take the left-hand branch. Towards the top, near the small waterfalls, is a sign indicating a left turn. Follow this, working up left slightly away from the stream to avoid impassable waterfalls. When the stream forks again, take the left branch up a small side valley on its left flank, following this to a bed of cotton grass and reeds. Continue NNE arriving at Fan Frynych summit.

5. From the summit head south, past the old quarry workings, and join the path by the side of the fence above Craig Cerrig-gleisiad. Follow this to a stile where another fence meets it from the west.

Craig Cerrig-gleisiad is the eastern part of the National Nature Reserve and is similar in character to Cwm-du (see D1). This is a good vantage point for taking photographs looking down into Craig Cerrig-gleisiad or for pictures of Corn Du and Pen y Fan in the distance to the east. There is a Countryside Council for Wales sign at this point.

6. Cross over the stile, turn right and follow the fence to the west. Continue, with the slope on the right becoming steeper all the time, until the high point of Craig Cwm-du is reached above the steepest crags.

From this vantage point above the crags are good views of Corn Du and Pen y Fan to the east and Fforest Fawr to the west (see D5). The bowl-shaped hill is Fan Gyhirych and to its right and beyond is Bannau Sir Gaer. The summit on its left with the trig point is Fan Nedd.

7. Leave the top of the crags and follow the track due south, arriving at a cairn just short of the summit of Fan Dringarth.

Below on the left there is evidence of a quarry (Geology of Brecon Beacons, see C1). Look out for a variety of upland birds (see C2).

8. Continue following the ridge SSW to the slightly higher summit of Fan Llia. A little further on are a number of peat pools and the site of an ancient cairn.

Looking due south, the prominent ridge in the distance is the Rhigos. Beyond the ridge, and hidden by it, are the South Wales mining valleys.

Fan Llia is covered by purple moor grass (*Molinia*) together with mat grass (*Nardus*) and heath rush (*Juncus squarrosus*). Soft rush (*Juncus effusus*) is common towards the southern end of the ridge. The peat pools are useful foreground for photographs of Corn Du and Pen y Fan.

9. The cairn provides a reference point to start the descent (SSW) to reach the stream of Afon Llia where the coniferous forestry fence drops down the hillside to the stream bed (GR 9264 1660).

10. Head upstream along the right-hand bank of the stream to Rhyd Uchaf.

11. Pick up the Sarn Helen Roman Road here and turn sharp left to return to the start.

D5. Fan Gyhirych/Fan Nedd

Start:	South of Maen Llia
Grid Reference:	9237 1905
Distance:	10km (6.4 miles)
Height Gained:	442m (1450ft)

These hills are part of Fforest Fawr and are more rounded and gentle than the high peaks of the Brecon Beacons. The walk includes the summits of Fan Gyhirych and Fan Nedd and, although of reasonable length, is not too strenuous. Ascents and descents are gentle but there

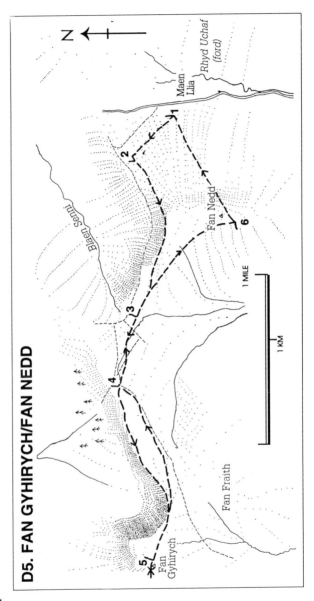

D5. FAN GYHIRYCH/FAN NEDD

may be some difficulty in route finding in bad weather as the tracks are unfrequented. This area is to be recommended if you like solitude and there are some fine views to be enjoyed in clear weather.

* * *

ROUTE

1. Start about 100m south of the standing stone, Maen Llia, on the western side of the road where there is a stile. Soon after crossing the stile, turn right (NW) and follow a collapsed stone wall diagonally across the hillside up to the right to where a path leads along a wire fence.

2. Turn left (SW) along this path which cuts across the face of Fan Nedd.

The valley lying before you is called Blaen Senni. This area is part of Fforest Fawr (see D5). As you turn the corner, the head of the valley becomes quite steep with a number of Brownstone crags leading down from the summit of Fan Nedd on the left (Geology of Brecons, C1). Before reaching the crags there is a fine panorama with sandstone blocks in the foreground, the head of the U-shaped valley in the middle-ground and Fan Gyhirych in the background (Glacial origin of U-shaped valleys A10). Looking back to the north, there is a patchwork landscape of fields and natural woodland.

Climbing the valley the impressive cliff and cusp of Fan Gyhirych may be seen. The hill up to the left beyond the wall is Fan Nedd. Look back occasionally for views of the summits of Corn Du and Pen y Fan in the distance.

At GR 9111 1911, cross the main gully which drains the slope above. This is attractive with heather and bilberry on either side and a few rowan trees. The whole of the bed of the gully is carpeted with turf and moss and is dry in the summer but a frothy stream in winter.

D5 Fforest Fawr, The Great Forest of Brecknock - The broad upland area between Pen y Fan in the east and Carmarthen Fan in the west is known as Fforest Fawr, the Great Forest. The term "Forest" is a legal definition and denotes an area of land set aside for royalty for hunting. Fforest Fawr came under Forest Law after the Norman Conquests of the Welsh Princes in 1066. The formerly wooded valleys provided good cover for game and, in particular, red deer, a truly royal beast and an important source of fresh venison during the winter. The semi-fortified enclosure of Castell Coch at the confluence of Afon Dringarth and Afon Llia was in the heart of the Forest and may well have been the site of the Forest Court where offenders were tried. By the beginning of the eighteenth century, the last deer had disappeared due to poaching and grazing competition with Commoners' flocks of sheep and herds of cattle. Fforest Fawr was split up by the Act of Enclosure 1815 and of the original 39,390 acres, 21,484 acres were withdrawn from the Common and sold to private landholders. The funds raised by the Crown were supposedly to finance wars but in fact they were used for the building of Regent Street in London.

The slope on the left eases and just before the col, join the permitted route which drops from the summit of Fan Nedd.

Continue to the col between the valleys of Blaen Senni and the Nedd.

3. **From the col follow the fence on your right.**

The col is quite boggy and can be very wet after a rainy period.

At the end of the col is a fence and gate with a white arrow indicating a permitted footpath. Follow this sign up to the left.

From this point, looking back down the Blaen Senni Valley, there are fine views into Cwm-du (see D3), the western half of a National Nature Reserve (see D1). The line at the top of the green fields is, more or less, where Sarn Helen, the Roman Road, runs and to the right of this the two highest peaks of the Brecon Beacons are clearly in view, Corn Du (Black Horn) to the right and Pen y Fan to the left.

About 15m past the gatepost, cross a derelict stone wall. Cut across the field, climbing diagonally up the slope to a wire fence. Follow this to the apex of fences.

The Rhigos mountain forms the skyline to the left.

Nearing the apex of this field, climb over the brow of the hill and directly ahead is a gate in the fence leading to an obvious track. This gate is signposted with a white permitted footpath arrow.

Beyond is the impressive sweeping cliff of Fan Gyhirych on the extreme western edge of the Central Brecon Beacons map. The owners of the land have put in new fences but unfortunately have left behind piles of rusting wire.

4. Go straight across the track as the route is made more interesting by skirting around the cwm above the headwall.

Coming over the brow of the hill can be seen the fine profile of Bannau Sir Gaer, the Carmarthen Fan. Below to the right is the Cray reservoir and in the foreground is a private forestry plantation.

D5 Moorland under threat - Overgrazing by sheep has resulted in a loss of heather moorland. This is replaced by bent and fescue grassland, often intermixed with mat grass. Our only deciduous grass, purple moor grass, grows in wetter areas such as the moor between Penderyn and the Mellte. Its dead leaves can be found trapped on wire fences after winter storms. Tragically, the Forestry Commission has attempted to drain and plant conifers here, causing considerable damage to peat bog habitat.

Looking back from this point, there is a good view of the Brecon Beacons.

The upper third part of the back slope of the cwm in front of Fan Gyhirych is marked by a resistant rock band which marks an abrupt change of slope.

As you follow the edge of the cwm, the ground to the right becomes much steeper. The surface on this side of the headwall of Fan Gyhirych has a crenulated appearance from the myriad sheep tracks that have crossed it horizontally. This imparts a kind of ripple effect as it is combined with soil creep. Some of the uppermost ledges are partly inaccessible to grazing sheep and have an interesting flora. Green spleenwort *(Asplenium viride)*, brittle bladder-fern *(Cystopteris fragilis)*, northern bedstraw *(Galium boreale)*, *Phegopteris connectilis* and cliff meadow rue *(Thalictrum minus)* are found here together with a collection of uncommon bryophytes found only in rocky upland areas.

From the rounded summit of Fan Gyhirych you look down to the Neath Valley (SW) with Pontneddfechan in the middle ground and the Rhigos massif in the background. On the far horizon, looking south of Fan Gyhirych, is the conspicuous smoke stack at Baglan Bay. The stretch of water to the right of this is Mumbles Bay. To the east is

Fan Nedd which has a steep slope to the left. Beyond, in the distance, are the Black Mountains to the left of Pen y Fan. Further to the left of Pen y Fan, you may see the town of Brecon.

From the top of the headwall, cross west to the trig point about 400m away.

Once at the trig point, look west for a good view of Fan Hir (the Long Ridge) which leads up to Bannau Sir Gaer. The summit is covered by peat on which grows hare's tail grass (*Eriophorum vaginatum*) mire. Common cotton-grass (*E. angustifolium*) can be found together with wavy hair grass (*Deschampsia flexuosa*) and heath rush (*Juncus squarrosus*).

5. Continue west of the trig point for a view over the Swansea Valley.

Down to the left are the spectacular limestone caves of Dan-yr-Ogof and the high land above is their catchment area. Below the caves can be seen, with the aid of binoculars, the house of Madam Adelina Patti, the famous opera soprano.

Fan Gyhirych is one of the finest panoramic viewpoints in South Wales.

Retrace your steps to the trig point at the summit and follow the permitted right of way down to the gate where you meet the obvious track again.

Retrace your outward route by turning right through a gate indicated by a white path arrow. Head downslope in the direction of Fan Nedd, returning to the col at the start of Section 3, and take the path which winds up the ridge to the trig point on the summit of Fan Nedd.

On the last few stretches of the climb, you come across a number of eroded peat haggs (see B5). Loss of peat here has been slowed down considerably by recolonising plants. Finally, the slope eases and you end up walking over *Nardus* grassland gently to the summit. Vegetation here is a mixture of hare's tail grass (*Eriophorum vaginatum*), mat grass (*Nardus*), bilberry (*Vaccinium myrtillus*) with frequent common cotton-grass (*E. angustifolium*), wavy hair grass (*Deschampsia flexuosa*) and some crowberry (*Empetrum nigrum*) growing on peat up to a metre deep.

6. From the summit of Fan Nedd take a bearing north-east and follow the track down to the road past the earthwork marked on the map. You meet the road opposite the standing stone of Maen Llia.

The north-east slope of Fan Nedd is carpeted in a springy cover of ling *(Calluna vulgaris)* in places. The standing stone is very impressive and well worth a visit.

D5 Maen Llia - This Bronze Age standing stone has served as a distinctive waymark for thousands of years.

Waterfall Country

E1. Pontneddfechan Waterfalls

Start:	Old White Horse Inn in Pontneddfechan
Grid Reference:	9015 0766
Distance:	8km (5 miles)

This is a low level walk around the beautiful riverside scenery of the Afon Pyrddin and the Afon Nedd. The route is easily followed and includes a number of impressive waterfalls. Autumn is the best season for a visit as the route is entirely through deciduous forestry. Paths are well marked and no great effort is required to complete the route, even in bad weather. The river geology is very interesting and there is evidence of old industrial and mining activity in the valley. After heavy rain the rivers are in spate and the waterfalls are at their best. The walk returns to the Old White Horse Inn where you will find a warm welcome, good food and drink.

✳ ✳ ✳

ROUTE
1. **From the Old White Horse Inn (Tafarn yr Hen Geffyl Gwyn) walk to the bridge across the Afon Nedd (River Neath). A wrought iron sign indicates that the path leads to the "White Lady Falls" (Sgwd Gwladus). Pass through the cast iron kissing gates and follow the wide track up the left (W) side of the river.**

There are good exposures of the rock strata on the far side of the river where the dip of the Millstone Grit beds to the south is clearly evident.

E1 The Travels of Giraldus Cambrensis - Giraldus Cambrensis, the son of a Norman Baron and a Welsh Princess, wrote *Itinerarium Cambriae* or *Journey of Wales* in the late twelfth century. He travelled around Wales, spreading propaganda supporting the Crusades, and recorded many interesting stories. One of these concerned Elidyr who lived in the upper Neath Valley in the fourth

---

E1. PONTNEDDFECHAN WATERFALLS

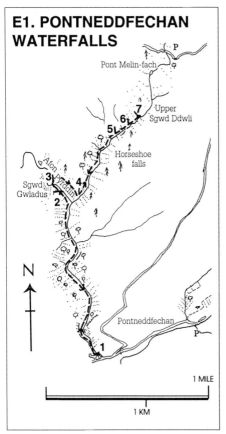

Pont Melin-fach

Upper Sgwd Ddwli

Horseshoe falls

Afon Pyrddin

Sgwd Gwladus

Afon Nedd

N

Pontneddfechan

1 MILE

1 KM

century. Elidyr was learning to read at the age of twelve but was frequently beaten by his disciplinarian teacher and, to escape his wrath, ran away and hid in a hollow along the banks of the Afon Nedd. After two days he was hungry and miserable but then two tiny men appeared who offered to take him to a land where all was play-time and pleasure. They led him through a dark underground tunnel to a beautiful country but it was rather dark as the sun did not shine here. The people of this world never lied and lived on a vegetarian diet. Elidyr became friends with the King's son but frequently returned to the upper world where he told only his mother of his adventures. His mother asked him to bring her back a present of gold, a common metal in the land. Elidyr returned with a golden ball which he stole while playing with the King's son. The little people caught up with him as he tripped on the doorstep of his house, snatching the ball and running off with it making remarks of scorn and derision to Elidyr. Realising his foolish act, Elidyr ran back to the river but the entrance to the underground tunnel had gone.

The track continues through hazel and sycamore past a number of old mill workings (one on the left with five granite mill stones) and drops back down to the river to an open clearing with picnic tables. The path is wide and good enough here for wheel chairs. It goes through a gate or stile where on the left is an old flooded mine working with three adits branching from the entrance.

On a hot summer's day the air in the tunnels is surprisingly cool but in the winter it feels warm and muggy. The reason for this is that the air in underground passages remains at a constant temperature of 4°C regardless of the season. Beyond, on the left, is a bricked entrance to another working and there are others on the far side of the river where a small side valley, Cwm Gored, branches off from here.

E1 Industry along the Nedd Fechan - The flooded adits that lead underground on the west side of the Nedd Fechan were once worked for silica by about 30 miners. These are just part of a more extensive system of mine workings on both sides of the river. Silica mining in the valley began in the early 1820s and carried on for nearly a hundred years. William Weston Young discovered how to make fire bricks from Dinas Silica which were used all over Europe and America to line iron and steel making furnaces, limekilns and domestic fire places. The rock was crushed in the valley and then transported by horse-drawn tram to the fire brick factory at Pont Walby, which closed in 1920. The hard sandstone was also used for making millstones. The remains of a double-race mill are passed on the left bank. This was used to grind corn grown by local farmers. Ddinas rock was quarried for limestone which was transported to Pont Walby where it was crushed and either heated to produce lime for agricultural use or used for road metalling.

The path narrows and climbs slightly up some wooden steps, clearly now not suitable for wheel chairs. After a short distance the confluence of the rivers is reached at a deep pool just below an iron footbridge.

2.   Do not cross the footbridge but continue north-west on the left bank of the Afon Pyrddin to a viewing platform before Sgwd Gwladus. If the river is low, scramble down to the stream bed and

pass carefully behind the fall, using boulders as stepping stones to gain the bank on the other side. These stones are submerged if the river is in spate and you will have to return to the bridge, cross it, and visit Sgwd Gwladus via the northern bank.

It is only reasonably possible to pass behind the fall when the river is not in flood. Under these conditions, the water comes over in a single spout on the extreme left-hand side of the bedding plane which forms the top of the fall, allowing a fairly dry passage. When the river is in spate, the fall comes down in a sheet which extends across to the right. After passing behind the fall, up above on the damp rock is an interesting collection of wet-loving plants such as ferns. The best viewpoints for photographs of the fall appear to be from the middle of the river below the viewing platform, or from the side before you walk around behind the fall. Photographic composition is difficult once you have passed behind the water.

E1 Sgwd Gwladus - Sgwd is Welsh for waterfall and comes from the verb ysgwd which means to toss or fling. This fall has been popular with tourists for many years and is known by English visitors as Lady Fall. The Welsh name comes from Gwladys, a daughter of the fifth-century King Brychan of Brycheiniog who had twenty-four daughters and twelve sons! Brychan was unusually, for

Geological cross-section Sgwd Gwladus

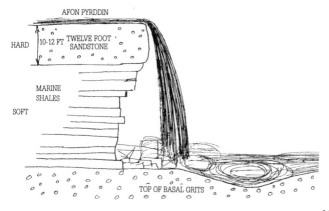

AFON PYRDDIN

HARD | 10-12 FT TWELVE FOOT SANDSTONE

MARINE SHALES

SOFT

TOP OF BASAL GRITS

his time, of Goidelic or Irish descent. Sgwd Gwladus occurs where the Afon Pryddin encounters a resistant band of Millstone Grit sandstone. The middle part of the geological formation known as the Millstone Grit consists mostly of black, crumbling shales but there are layers of hard sandstone, the most important of which is the "twelve foot sandstone" which occurs 13m above the base of the shale division. The general level of the Pyrddin is above the surface of this massive band of grit. Upstream of Sgwd Gwladus, the Pyrddin rapidly cut a steep gorge through the weak upper shales, the floor of the gorge being, for some distance, the surface of the 12ft sandstone itself. The black shales exposed in the face of the fall are easily eroded by water and, from time to time, blocks of the overhanging massive sandstone bed become undermined so much that they collapse. The waterfall is slowly migrating upstream as a result, as well as laterally to the west due to the inclination of the strata in this direction. In dry conditions, the water comes over the extreme left side of the bedding plane which forms the top of the fall. When the river is in spate, the fall comes down in a single sheet which extends across to the right.

3. Climb up above the fall to the "rocking stone", a large boulder in the river bed, which has unfortunately been vandalised and is now immobile. The right bank can be explored for only a short distance upstream before it becomes impassable without wading the river. From here follow the eastern bank downstream back to the bridge.

This is a popular place in warm weather with swimmers dropping into the pool below from a rope swing.

4. Back at the bridge do not cross it but follow the left bank of the left-hand tributary, the Nedd Fechan (Little Neath).

This path takes you high above the gorge which has a number of small waterfalls (Rivers of the Waterfall Country, see E2).

In a short distance, the path falls to the level of the river where there are a number of rapids. On the left side, near these falls, is a lovely small stream cascading over moss covered rocks. As you follow the bend from the rapids, deep river pools can be seen and above these are the photogenic and aptly named Horseshoe Falls.

The Horseshoe Falls on the Afon Nedd

Photography is best here in summer since the low winter sun is obscured for most of the day by the steep valley sides.

5. Above the Horseshoe Falls are the Lower and Upper Sgwd Ddwli (waterfalls). Approach the Lower either via the flat rocks in the river bed (if the water is low) or by a track up to the left if they are covered.

The Lower Sgwd Ddwli falls are in two sections, the second part being higher than the first and in an enclosed cliff area.

6. To continue upstream from Lower Sgwd Ddwli retrace your steps along the stream bed. Walk about 20m to the end of the crags (above to the right) and scramble up the slope to gain the path above. About 50m above Lower Sgwd Ddwli is a pool about 6m in depth which was once cut by the Upper Sgwd Ddwli waterfall. This fall is some 200m further upstream around a bend in the river.

The Upper Sgwd Ddwli is very photogenic and is illuminated

best by early afternoon light. If you are lucky, a dipper may pose in the foreground (Birds of the Waterfall Country, see E4).

7. Retrace your steps to the iron footbridge and back down the western bank of the Afon Nedd (River Neath) to Pontneddfechan.

E2. Waterfall Walk

Start:	Pontneddfechan
Grid Reference:	9015 0766
Distance:	18km (11.2 miles)

This is a low level walk around the beautiful riverside scenery of the Afon Pyrddin, Afon Nedd, Afon Mellte and the Afon Hepste. The route is well defined and includes a number of impressive waterfalls. Autumn is the best season for a visit as the route is mostly through deciduous forestry but during exceptionally hard winters the waterfalls freeze, providing some spectacular scenes. Although not strenuous in terms of ascents or descents, the distance covered is considerable and the ground may be rough and slippery so that progress is slow. Some of the finest river scenery in South Wales is to be enjoyed and the walk is highly recommended.

* * *

ROUTE
The first part of this walk follows sections 1-6 of Route E1 as far as the Upper Sgwd Ddwli waterfall.

7. After the falls, the gorge is left behind. Follow a grassy path along the western bank of the river with a wire fence on the left. In a short distance, cross a stile leading to a picnic area.

8. Cross the grassed picnic area to the car park and onto the road. Turn right across Pont Melin-fach (Small Mill Bridge) and follow the road up the hill, ignoring the stile on the left just over the bridge.

9. At the next farmyard gate on the left, there is a house (Glyn-

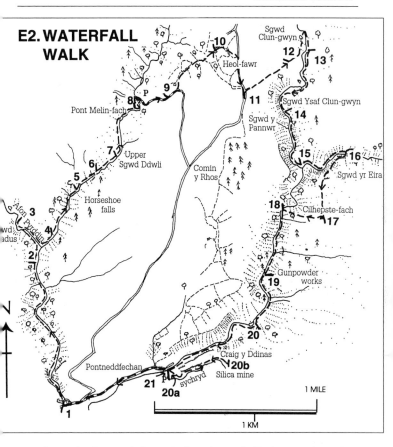

E2. WATERFALL WALK

Sgwd Clun-gwyn

Heol-fawr

Pont Melin-fach

Sgwd Ysaf Clun-gwyn

Sgwd y Pannwr

Upper Sgwd Ddwli

Comin y Rhos

Sgwd yr Eira

Horseshoe falls

Afon Pyrddin

Cilhepste-fach

Gunpowder works

Craig y Ddinas

Pontneddfechan

sychryd

Silica mine

N

1 MILE

1 KM

mercher-uchaf). Turn left just before the road climbs steeply and go
through the gate to the right of the house. Continue along an old
farm track with a stone wall on either side planted with trees. Take
the right-hand fork along a conspicuous track. The old farm lane
you are following has a wire fence on the left and an old field
boundary on the right with an improved field beyond.

After about a hundred metres, the track bears left to a gate.
Continue along this to a second gate and follow the track to the

167

farm, Heol-fawr. **Before the farm buildings on the right, pass through a gate to a tarmac lane.**

10. Where the lane turns sharp left, turn right along a muddy farm track to a stile on the left. Cross this and aim straight across the field to a stile opposite a church. Turn right down the road passing a small shop on the right and a garage with a telephone box on the left. Continue down the road, crossing a cattle grid and just after this on the left is a limestone chipping car park. An information board to the Waterfall Country marks the start of a track which leads between stone walls.

11. Proceed down the stony lane and after about 60m, cross over a small stream and follow the National Park yellow signs which direct you right at a fork in the track. Pass through a field and then cross a stile before entering deciduous woodland.

Soon you will hear the roar of the Mellte as it plunges over the waterfall of Sgwd Clun-gwyn.

Drop through the woods to a junction of paths with the waterfall straight ahead. Ignore the turning back to the right and continue left along the western bank to the top of the waterfall, Sgwd Clun-gwyn. Descend the steep slope to the top of the fall.

The deep pools above the fall are ideal for a refreshing dip on warm summer days.

E2 Sgwd Clun-gwyn (White Meadow Fall) - Sgwd Clun-gwyn is found on the Afon Mellte where it tumbles over a resistant massive band of Millstone Grit sandstone. The lower parts of the fall can be explored by scrambling down its side using tree roots and good rock handholds to a middle terrace and then down to the stream bed. When only a little water is flowing, it is possible to walk along the middle terrace for a closer look at the mosses and ferns which thrive in this very damp environment. A deep trough has been carved at the bottom of the fall by the tremendous scouring power of the falling water.

Formation - The fall was formed by earth movements bringing shales of the middle Millstone Grit into contact with the pebbly grit that constitutes the lowest stratigraphical member of the same

---

Geological formation of Sgwyd Clun-Gwyn

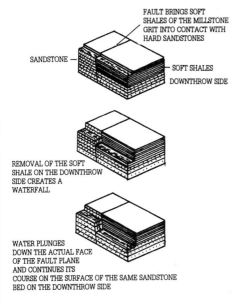

FAULT BRINGS SOFT SHALES OF THE MILLSTONE GRIT INTO CONTACT WITH HARD SANDSTONES

SANDSTONE

SOFT SHALES

DOWNTHROW SIDE

REMOVAL OF THE SOFT SHALE ON THE DOWNTHROW SIDE CREATES A WATERFALL

WATER PLUNGES DOWN THE ACTUAL FACE OF THE FAULT PLANE AND CONTINUES ITS COURSE ON THE SURFACE OF THE SAME SANDSTONE BED ON THE DOWNTHROW SIDE

formation. The weak shales are downstream of this geological fault which now forms the near vertical face of the waterfall. This same fault crosses the Hepste around a kilometre to the south-south-east but the amount of earth movement dies out in this direction and an obvious feature has not formed in the Hepste. The shales were rapidly eroded by tumbling water and have, in fact, been removed completely downstream of the fall as the river now runs across the same sandstone surface below the fall as it does above. This massive band of sandstone, known as the "twelve foot sandstone", is the same as the overhanging bed over which Sgwd Gwladus plunges (see E1). The fall has been working its way to the east as the tilt of the sandstone bedding forces the water in this direction. A cross-section of the fault can be found clearly exposed on the eastern bank in line with the top of the waterfall. A good view of this can be found from the opposite bank immediately above the lip of the fall but foliage may obscure this. Looking along the line of the fall, you will see a deep narrow gully in the opposite bank. The weak shales on the right of the fault, the downthrown side, have suffered considerable disruption whereas the competent massive sandstone bed on the left, the upthrown side, has suffered little internal fracturing. Shattering of the shales for some distance adjacent to the fault further reduced their ability to withstand erosion. The fact that the fault plane which forms the face of the waterfall is still in line with the trace of the fault in the bank means that Sgwd Clun-gwyn has, unusually, not migrated upstream since its inception, in stark contrast with Sgwd yr Eira (see E3).

Photography - This fall is very difficult to photograph. We have found two angles that work well from a compositional viewpoint. The first of these is from a classic high vantage point on the eastern bank. The second is a side profile from the middle terrace. The falls are well lit by an early afternoon sun. Pictures from below the falls are difficult because of high contrast between water and dark green foliage and also because of the need to wade into the river to achieve a satisfactory viewpoint. The best season for pictures is autumn when the leaves turn to colourful oranges, browns and reds, reducing contrast and adding greatly to photographic interest.

12. From the top of Sgwd Clun-gwyn, the adventurous can leap across the river just above the fall where the water runs in a narrow channel. If the river is in spate, walk upstream a few hundred metres to a bridge.

Cross this, turn right, and follow the east bank through woodland keeping as close to the river bed as possible. A narrow path with steep drops on the right skirts beneath an outcrop of Millstone Grit to a good vantage point above the fall.

Continue along the distinct path to the next falls.

13. At the top of Sgwd Isaf Clun-gwyn, climb down in front of the cliff where it is possible to walk along the edge to look at the upper cascade. Scramble around by the side of the pools and the falls. Descend to the lower pool of this sequence of falls and follow the bank of the river downstream.

E2 Sgwd Isaf Clun-gwyn (see p2) - This complex of cascades was formed by two parallel faults, fractures in the earth's crust, that brought a long narrow band of pebbly sandstones to the surface. The Mellte generally flows north to south along the outcrop of the middle shales of the Millstone Grit but the band of pebbly sandstone deflects its course to the west, crossing the sandstone by the

Sgwd Clun-gwyn taken along the line of the fault

shortest route and then turning south again once on a narrow tract of shale between the Farewell Rock (the Upper Millstone Grit sandstone) to the west and pebbly sandstone to the east. This present course is anomalous as the river would not change direction to the west in order to cross a resistant band of rock when by

171

> continuing due south it would stay on weaker shales. The likely explanation for this strange course is that it was predetermined by a fault in the shale which overlay the faulted wedge of grit. This shale was then removed by erosion but the stream continued to flow in the same direction, a phenomenon known as "superimposed" drainage.

Below the falls, there is a wide picnic area and the ground on the east of the river is quite flat. On the right-hand side is a very steep cliff.

Proceed down the river to another small fall, Sgwd y Pannwr (Fall of the Fuller).

In front of the falls is an oak tree.

14. Continue down the valley by leaving the fall via a path which drops down the slope from the left and crosses Millstone Grit boulders. Shortly, turn right, crossing more boulders, along a distinct path which climbs diagonally up the slope. The path narrows and runs three-quarters of the way up the side of the gorge and care is needed as there are precipitous drops to the stream bed far below.

From this path there are wonderful views looking down to where the river bed becomes quite wide in places. The path is steep and hard and the public right of way along the top of the gorge is easier to follow.

Once round the bend in the river, follow the path which drops to the river bed.

An easier route climbs to the top of the gorge and follows it to the junction of a number of paths. Continue straight on and follow the path which swings around to the left and into the Hepste Valley.

This drops through woodland to the base of a Millstone Grit cliff (Geological Rock Formations of the Waterfall Country, see E5). Below is the end of a series of cascades. Down to the right, there are some small falls and the gorge becomes much narrower again.

The path descends to river level and continues along the eastern bank to the confluence of the Afon Mellte and the Afon Hepste joining from the left.

15. **Once at the confluence of the rivers, climb the steep prow ahead, as the Hepste gorge which swings around to the left is impassable at river level. This slippery climb can be avoided by staying on the top of the gorge instead of dropping to the stream bed. A path leads across about half way up the slope. This joins the main path which zigzags its way down from the top. Follow this and drop down to the river bed again.**

During March, April and May the striking white blossom of the blackthorn is very noticeable when you are walking through the woodland.

The path descends to the river on a grassy bank then cuts up left via the river bed. Beyond this grassy bank, there is a series of falls in a narrow gorge.

These are the Lower Cilhepste Falls (see E4).

Pass these by climbing up to the left and continue upstream.

It is quite a steep climb up the rock to get to the left of these falls above the main ones.

Keep close to the river past these last three cascades. Turn the corner and in front is the waterfall, Sgwd yr Eira. The path scrambles up over the stones on the left bank (looking upstream) and then passes behind the cascade.

If there is a lot of water flowing, the wall on the left is quite wet and waterproofs are recommended (Sgwd yr Eira, see E3).

16. **After passing behind Sgwd yr Eira, the path leads up the steep slope to the left. Part of this climb is a bouldery stream bed but then towards the top there is a man-made zigzag of wooden ledges and posts. Don't deviate to the left but take the steps to the right following a small valley in the side of the main gorge. The path doubles back on itself, arriving at the edge of some coniferous forestry where there are large stone boulders. The track to the left goes towards Penderyn but take the path to the right along the top of the gorge.**

The path which ascends the steep gully has a geological fault running through it which was responsible for the original formation of the waterfall, which has since retreated upstream. The boulders at the top of the gully are glacial erratics and were transported by ice from another area and then left behind when the ice melted and the glacier retreated.

Walking along this well-cleared path, look down into the beautifully wooded gorge and the confluence of the two rivers. This piece of rather interesting land, which is owned by the Forestry Commission, is marked by a post sunk into the ground with a white band around it.

E2 Ancient woodland - Woodland clinging to the gorge walls of the Afon Mellte, Hepste, Sychryd, Nedd and Pyrddin forms one of the richest and most extensive areas of ancient semi-natural woodland in Wales. A wide variety of botanical types have been identified, ten in all, ranging from ash-maple woods on limestone to sessile oak-downy birch-wood sorrel types on Millstone Grit (Geological rock formations of the Waterfall Country, see E5). Downy birch-purple moor grass and alder-ash woods are found on wet ground conditions. Wet flushes in this type of woodland provide a home for marsh hawk's-beard *(Crepis paludosa)*, interestingly its most southerly locality in Britain. The sheer steepness and inaccessibility of the gorge walls have prevented timber exploitation in the past leaving an ancient woodland almost untouched by man in places. Only small pockets of truly ancient woodland survive today in Britain. Small-leaved lime thrives on cliff edges and steep slopes and is found together with wood fescue grass *(Festuca altissima)*. The undisturbed nature of the woodland means that it still has its rich complement of woodland associated species. This includes a number of rare ferns such as Wilson's filmy fern *(Hymenophyllum wilsonii)*, Tunbridge filmy fern *(H. tunbrigense)*, hay scented fern *(Dryopteris aemula)* and rare liverworts, mosses and lichens. These are found in a variety of habitats such as boulder scree, cliff faces, springs, decaying wood, ancient trees and numerous niches associated with streams and rivers.

The path leaves the top of the gorge and heads south.

The hill ahead in the distance is the Rhigos mountain, with a number of glacial corries in it. Beyond it is the South Wales Coalfield. The valley to the south-west is the Neath.

17. The route swings right and down towards the gorge around the

ruins of Cilhepste-fach. At this point, leave the waymarked footpath following the ride which runs west through the coniferous forestry. Beyond the forestry, pick up the line of a collapsed stone wall and look out for a conspicuous oak tree near the edge of the gorge at the end of a spur of land. This marks the beginning of the steep descent of an ill-defined zigzag path to an easy path along the eastern bank of the river below. Turn left on reaching this path.

18. Follow this distinct path downstream to the last waterfall on the Hepste which is in two tiers. Continue downstream past a small brick structure and on to the old gunpowder works where there is a weir.

The extensive collection of ruined buildings, weirs and leats in the lower reaches of the valley were once a gunpowder works (see E4).

E2 Rivers of the Waterfall Country - The rivers of the Waterfall Country, the Mellte, Hepste, Sychryd, Pyrddin and the upper parts of the Neath, flowed into the Cynon Valley to the south-west. Earth movements during late Tertiary times uplifted this area, accelerating the rate at which South Wales rivers were cutting valleys. The River Neath was particularly "rejuvenated" and greatly extended its course north-east utilising a line of weakness along a narrow belt of greatly folded and faulted rocks, the Neath Disturbance. The River Neath managed to capture the rivers of the Waterfall Country so that they flowed faster into the lower levels of the Neath. The rejuvenated rivers cut steep-sided gorges as waterfalls receded upstream.

---

19. From the weir, a well-made path continues along the side of the river, which is now quite wide. The path arrives at a flat area with some pleasant old woodland. Beyond the flat boggy area, where alder grows, is a constriction in the river. In the middle of the river bed is a block of rock which is tilted at about 45° towards the west. As you cross over the top of this, the path is obstructed on the left by a crumbling structure. In front of you is a wooden bridge. Scramble up the side of these broken-down blocks or make a detour to the left to get back to the path.

20. Do not cross the wooden bridge but head straight across the

grassy meander ahead to gain a distinct path along the side of the river. Continue past a stilling station on the far bank. Follow the track down to the bridge and the impressive cliff of Craig y Ddinas.

An old tram route ran past Craig y Ddinas connecting the silica mine with the Vale of Neath Canal (Craig y Ddinas, see E3; Industry Along the Nedd Fechan, see E1).

** EXTENSION LEAVES FROM HERE **

21. From Craig y Ddinas, follow the road out of the car park across the river and walk back to the start in Pontneddfechan.

** EXTENSION **

20a. From Craig y Ddinas, there is an option of visiting the Sychryd Valley with its waterfalls and silica mines. Go into the car park and follow the footpath leading to the right of the crags. Walk into the narrow gorge with the stream below on the right. Rounding the corner, pass below an impressive cliff.

Further up, this gorge becomes very narrow and the river tumbles down over a series of rocks. The impressive rock exposure at the entrance to the gorge on the right is called Bwa Maen (see E3).

The gorge becomes impassable at this point, and you have to back-track a little way and take the path which climbs high up to the left and traverses across the cliff. Continue along the path through the gorge and up to the silica mines and a waterfall. This route is quite exposed in places and is only for the more adventurous. Alternatively, if the river is fairly low, jump across a few boulders and cross to the other side in front of the main cliff and then scramble up on the right-hand side. Follow the path up a little wooded cwm where there is an old quarry.

20b. From here, climb left up the path to meet the Ridgeway and turn left down the hill to Craig y Ddinas. Join the main Route E1 and so return to the start in Pontneddfechan.

E3. Sgwd yr Eira

Start:	Penderyn
Grid Reference:	9448 0890
Distance:	10km (6 miles)

Here is an excellent walk, packed full of interest, culminating in an unforgettable experience of walking behind a waterfall. An initial easy ascent of Moel Penderyn is followed by an exploration of the Sychryd and Hepste Valleys where you will see evidence of a busy industrial past. Old ruins are left behind as you wind your way through the picturesque Hepste gorge with its tumbling river and steep slopes covered in ancient woodland. The best is left to the last when you climb out of the Hepste Valley and drop into the Mellte gorge and walk behind Sgwd yr Eira, the Fall of Snow. The paths are reasonably easy to follow and there are good views in the early part of the walk followed by spectacular river scenery. The Red Lion, a few hundred metres south of the end of this walk, is full of character with fine ales and open fires.

* * *

ROUTE

1. From Penderyn take the track (W) towards the old quarries, through a gate with the distinctive yellow National Park arrow marking the route. Continue straight ahead to another gate and cross the stile. Turn immediately left following the hill fence leaving some quarry spoils on your right. Work up to the col ahead and then leave the fence and cross west to the summit of Moel Penderyn marked by a trig point.

North and slightly west from here you can see Fan Nedd with the Carmarthen Fans further to the west. North-east are the Brecon Beacons. To the west of the road is the line of the Afon Hepste and to the east are the hills of Cefn Cadlan. There are many clues on the map as to the rock type of this area such as numerous "Areas of Shake Holes" and "Swallow Holes". These are typical of limestone country and, in fact, this area is a honeycomb of underground passages. The limestone is mostly capped by a layer of Millstone Grit. Swallow holes literally "swallow" streams when they disappear underground whereas shake holes are formed when the roof of an underground chamber or passage caves in. In this area, the Millstone Grit has often collapsed when the limestone beneath has been dissolved away. The Afon Hepste has changed its underground course many times, moving further south and west, leaving behind an extensive system of caves with spectacular stalagmites and stalactites.

E3 Limestone - Limestone is mainly composed of calcium carbonate which is slightly soluble in water. Limestone is more vigorously dissolved if weak acids are present in the water. In fact, ground water which formed remarkable cave systems in South Wales is slightly acidic due to acid rain and from humic acids produced in soil and from the breakdown of coniferous pine needles.

To the east is the massive limestone quarry (Cwar Llwyn-on) overlooking the village. South-east of it is the storage tank for North Sea gas. To the south-east is the Cynon Valley and over to the south-west is the Rhigos Mountain with open cast coal mines on its flanks. Beyond and due west is the Swansea Valley.

2. Walk due west along the crest of the ridge.

A close look at the rock outcrops here reveals that the limestone pavement has been polished by water, indicating that this area once suffered the powerful scouring action of a stream. Moel Penderyn is also geologically interesting for a different reason. Compressive forces in the earth's crust have pushed the rock strata

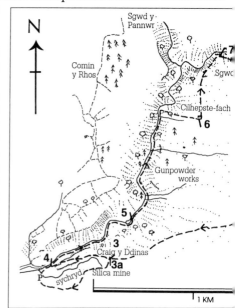

into the form of an elongated dome, technically known as a pericline. The axis of this fold, known as the Penderyn Anticline, runs for many kilometres north-eastwards into the Old Red Sandstone and south-westwards into the coal measures (Geology of Brecon Beacons, see C1; Old Red Sandstone, see B3). This fold was formed during the Caledonian mountain building period as a result of north-westward compression. Beyond the ridge is a bilberry and cotton grass heath.

E3 Earth movements - Mountain building earth movements which took place at the base of the Old Red Sandstone and at the end of the Upper Palaeozoic have been named the Caledonian and Hercynian, respectively. Caledonian movements spanned a time interval of more than 100 million years, at least from latest Cambrian to post-Silurian, and were responsible for folding and faulting of rocks resulting in geological structures aligned in a north-east south-west direction. After these mid-Devonian movements died away, there was little mountain building until late Carboniferous times. At the end of the Coal Measures, the Brecon Beacons were on the southern flanks of a southward moving continent which eventually collided with a northward moving land mass to the south. Enormous compressive forces caused strong folding and faulting of Upper Palaeozoic rocks. The outstanding feature that resulted from these tectonic movements is the syncline of the South Wales coalfield and the regional southward tilt of the rocks of the Brecon Beacons originated as part of its northern limb. A major structure disrupts the northern rim of the coalfield and runs through the lower parts of the Waterfall Country. This is a complex fault system known as the Neath Disturbance which grew intermittently from Dinantian times, reaching its zenith in late-Carboniferous times.

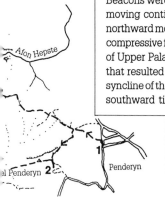

E3. SGWD YR EIRA

Drop left before you reach a forestry fence to a track, known as the Ridgeway, which connected Penderyn with Pontneddfechan.

The Ridgeway is an old drovers' road (see D4).

Follow this through a gate, heading in the direction of the head of the Neath Valley, dropping over the brow of the hill. Pass the ruins of Clwyd-rhyd-fan to reach mixed woodland. The track winds between spoil-heaps from old silica mines to a wooden sign with a marker pointing back to Penderyn.

Looking back you can see the entrance to some of the mines.

3. At this point you can either take the rising track ahead to Craig y Ddinas or take the path off to the left signposted to the silica mines.

** EXTENSION LEAVES FROM HERE **

4. From Craig y Ddinas take the path north-east, signposted to the gunpowder works. This travels along the eastern bank of the Afon Mellte to a man-made weir with a cable strung across the river.

The building on the opposite bank contains a stilling well which is used for measuring the height of the river (Rivers of the Waterfall Country, see E2).

Continue along the path through woodland to a small open area where an obvious path goes up to the right. Ignore this and follow the river bank to a wooden bridge.

5. A sign points to the gunpowder works over the bridge and a direction marker indicates a route to the silica mines up some steps to the right. Ignore these, continuing up the eastern bank, scrambling down a wall near a small fall. When the bank steepens, the path climbs to the right and then descends to the river at an open area where gunpowder workings can be seen on the far bank. Beyond is a sluice which you pass on your left.

In the river are remnants of an old bridge. At the northern end of the sluice is a weir (Gunpowder Works, see E4).

Continue upstream past old gunpowder workings on the right. Begin to climb past a ruined building on the left to the first waterfall which has two tiers. The path climbs above it, crossing a

steep sided valley.

There are striking iron pigmented rocks below in the river.

Eventually the path reaches a high point but do not descend where the path drops to river level before the river swings into a left-hand bend. At the high point on the path is a steep, grassy, wooded slope leading up to the horizon. Make your way up this steep slope past an oak tree passing a small rock outcrop on the right side. There is no clear path at first but keep on the arête of the hill meeting a path which zigzags up to a large oak tree on the left. From here continue due east to coniferous forestry on the right. Follow a low stone wall on the left which meets the track from Craig y Ddinas at Cilhepste-fach.

6. Continue ahead, following the yellow arrow on the left and then white arrows to the left across deforested land. The track bears slightly right when it meets the Hepste Valley.

Look carefully here to find orchids flowering in spring and summer.

The path soon comes to some large boulders which mark the start of a descent left down wooden steps to Sgwd yr Eira.

These boulders are glacial erratics which were transported by ice from the north and then left behind when the ice melted and the glacier retreated. The path descends to a steep gully which formed due to a geological fault running through it which weakened the rock. This fault was also responsible for the original formation of the waterfall which has since retreated upstream.

E3 Sgwd yr Eira - This is the most exciting to visit of all the falls in the Brecon Beacons National Park. It provides the unforgettable experience of walking behind a moving curtain of thundering water. The character of the fall is the result of the local geology. Notice when you stand behind the fall that your feet are on hard sandstone but that the rocks in a one and a half metre recessed band at the base of the cliff are relatively weak, thinly bedded shales that crumble away easily. This band is very conspicuous as it is covered in wet-loving vegetation. The rocks above are of a more resistant sandstone but are weakened by numerous bedding planes. The final massive band of sandstone which forms the protruding shelf over which the

---

water tumbles is the strongest and so is the most resistant to collapse, resulting in the fall being thrown out spectacularly into space. The fall developed where a geological fault caused the river to flow from hard sandstone on to soft shales. Removal of the shales undermines the sandstone beds above causing the waterfall to mig-

Geological formation of Sgwd yr Eira

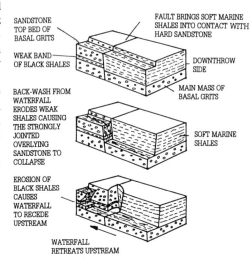

SANDSTONE TOP BED OF BASAL GRITS

FAULT BRINGS SOFT MARINE SHALES INTO CONTACT WITH HARD SANDSTONE

WEAK BAND OF BLACK SHALES

DOWNTHROW SIDE

MAIN MASS OF BASAL GRITS

BACK-WASH FROM WATERFALL ERODES WEAK SHALES CAUSING THE STRONGLY JOINTED OVERLYING SANDSTONE TO COLLAPSE

SOFT MARINE SHALES

EROSION OF BLACK SHALES CAUSES WATERFALL TO RECEDE UPSTREAM

WATERFALL RETREATS UPSTREAM

rate upstream, now over 70m from where the fault crosses the gorge. This point is marked by a gully in the southern side of the gorge which formed in response to weakening of the rocks by movement along the fault. This fall shares many characteristics in its formation with the famous Niagara Falls. Amazingly, the fall has frozen in severe winters. Adventurous canoeists have actually shot this fall and, for a short time, the record for the highest drop by canoe in Britain was held here.

Photography - This is a photogenic fall with a wide and unusual range of compositions. The fall faces almost due west and so is well lit by an afternoon sun. Standard shots include vertical and landscape formats taken from good vantage points on the steep southern slope of the gorge. An attractive small rainbow forms from the spray at the bottom of the fall in good lighting. Similar pictures can be taken from the northern bank. Fellow walkers can be positioned either behind or to the sides, adding interest and, more importantly, scale. More technically demanding and exciting shots can be taken from behind the curtain of water itself. Light shining through the water onto the

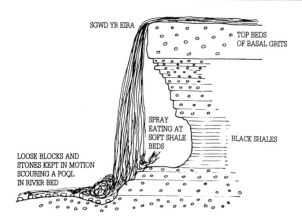

SGWD YR EIRA

TOP BEDS
OF BASAL GRITS

SPRAY
EATING AT
SOFT SHALE
BEDS

BLACK SHALES

LOOSE BLOCKS AND
STONES KEPT IN MOTION
SCOURING A POOL
IN RIVER BED

Geological cross-section through Sgwd yr Eira

back wall illuminates the brilliant green hues of the encrusting
vegetation. Pointing the lens directly at an afternoon sun creates an
interesting silhouette of trees and the rock shelf over which the river
is thrown.

**7.   After exploring behind the waterfall, return up the steps to the
boulders and bear left along an obvious path following the top of
the wooded gorge to a stile. A yellow National Park arrow directs
you along the right of a fence past a warning sign concerning the
dangers of the Waterfall Country. This waymarked path brings you
back to the start in Penderyn.**

** EXTENSION **

**3a. At the end of Section 2 of the main route, take the left turn
signposted to the silica mines, down wooden steps to the concrete
platforms by the river.**
EITHER **- take the track down the right of the stream (avoiding the
bridge) which takes you below an impressive overhanging cliff
and narrows to a ledge which intrepid walkers can descend with
care to the river.**

A good head for heights is needed and from here follow the

path along the Afon Sychryd to Craig y Ddinas.

From here you can see Bwa Maen, the impressive fold in the limestone on the other side of the river.

E3 Bwa Maen - The Welsh name means "bow rock" and well describes the spectacularly exposed arch-like fold with a sharp crest. If you look closely at the large boulders that have fallen from the roof of a cave, you will see that the rounded convex surfaces have small grooves. These are formed by the beds of rock rubbing together when they were being folded. The Carboniferous limestone was squeezed into this contorted feature by Amorican earth movements associated with the Neath Disturbance. A fault occurs immediately to the left of Bwa Maen along which the Sychryd now flows.

Geological cross-section through Craig y Ddinas and Bwa Maen

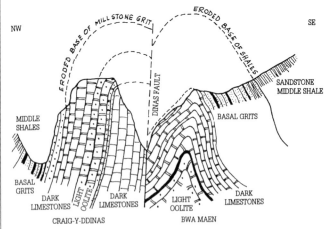

E3 Craig y Ddinas (Rock Fort) - This 50m high limestone cliff is of great geological significance as the continuation of the Vale of Neath Disturbance runs through it. The contorted limestone strata here are the surface evidence of enormous crustal earth movements which took place along lines of weakness known as geological faults. The tilted limestone beds of the near vertical face provide challenging rock routes whereas the easy cliffs to its right are popular with beginners learning to climb and abseil. Legend claims that the rock is the final resting place of King Arthur and the Knights of the Round Table.

OR - **cross the river bridge by the silica mines and climb to the right onto the ridge through oak, beech and hawthorn woodland to a large concrete block on the right with metal stansions let into it.**

These concrete stansions are all that remains of an unusual aerial ropeway used to transport stone from the mine to level ground near to Craig y Ddinas.

Don't take the steep path that drops to the river but swing left on the ridge and follow the path down through woodland and bracken to a metalled lane. Continue down right to Craig y Ddinas and the car park at the start of Section 4 of the main route.

E4. Ystradfellte Falls

Start:	Coed y Rhaiadr Forestry Commission car park
Grid Reference:	9175 1025
Distance:	14km (8.7 miles)

The Ystradfellte Waterfall Country has been famous for its natural beauty for many years. This varied route visits the spectacular waterfalls and steep wooded gorges of this area, taking in true ancient woodland, a rich industrial past and excellent geological and geomorphological features. It is quite a long walk along muddy and sometimes slippery river paths but there should be no difficulty in route finding if directions are carefully followed.

✳ ✳ ✳

ROUTE
1. **From the car park take the signposted footpath "Comin y Rhos" (Moorland Common) which cuts SSW across the field to the corner of the coniferous forestry. If this is too wet to cross, walk down the road, leaving it where a road leaves to the right and take the path to the left across the common to pick up the route at the far corner of the conifer plantation where there is a gate in a fence. Turn right at**

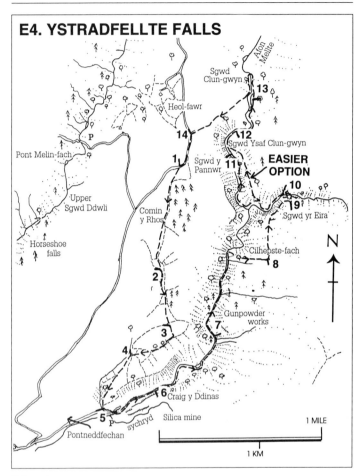

E4. YSTRADFELLTE FALLS

Afon Mellte

Sgwd Clun-gwyn **13**

Heol-fawr

14

12
Sgwd Ysaf Clun-gwyn

P

Pont Melin-fach

1
Sgwd y Pannwr **11**

EASIER OPTION

10

19

Upper Sgwd Ddwli

Comin y Rhos

Sgwd yr Eira

Horseshoe falls

2

Cilhepste-fach

8

3

Gunpowder works

7

4

6 Craig y Ddinas

5 P
sychryd   Silica mine

Pontneddfechan

N

1 MILE

1 KM

this gate.

Cross over a stile marked with a yellow National Park arrow, just after Carn y Crochan. Continue following the ditch on the left across a field with gorse, silver birch and alder to your left. On the right you can see the farm buildings of Pentre-d'rysgoed. Cross this field and over a stile, keeping the ditch on the left, where you pick up the farm track which after about 60m goes down to a gate with another yellow arrow.

2.   Immediately through the gate turn left to the bank of the stream and regain the right of way with the old wall on the right. Shortly, join the farm track and continue down it to a large gate. Beyond this, keep on the track which crosses poor grazing land and runs through a gap in a wall at two solid fence posts.

3.   Bear right, south-west, along the south side of the wall by field maple, mountain ash and hawthorn to the junction of several walls.
    You may be lucky enough to see curlew here.
    Head across the bracken covered field ahead in a south-westerly direction to a junction of several collapsed stone walls. Continue in the same direction following the wall which leads down the crest of the ridge in the direction of the Neath Valley. The wall more or less disappears but from here you will be able to see the boundary of the golf course. From this point, cut right to a stile in this wall at the apex of the course, marked by a small viewing tower.

4.   Cross over the stile and proceed along the right of way with a stone wall to the right. From the most southerly tip of this path, before it bends to the right and into the valley, make for the spur of land between a golf tee and green where there are wooden electricity poles. Continue to a stile with a yellow waymarker and drop down the wooded spur, bearing sharply right to a stream on the right and so to some houses.

5.   Turn left round the front of the houses and to the right is a sign to a picnic area. Cross the river on the road bridge below which is the confluence of the Mellte and the Sychryd rivers. Turn left with Craig y Ddinas straight ahead.
    On the left of the crag is an advised path sign, but just before the crag take a small path down to the left to the river bed where there is a sign for "Gunpowder Works".
    Down to the left of the Afon Mellte and just beyond is a steep bank which divides the river from a large lagoon.
    Follow the path which drops to river level.

The path passes through mainly hazel, birch and ash woodland (Ancient Woodland, see E2). It then climbs again leaving a steep drop to the water below. Further evidence of this area's industrial past can be seen on the opposite side of the river where there is a man-made sluice.

6. About a kilometre from the crag is a weir where there is a steel cable crossing from a stilling well on the opposite bank. This is used to measure the rise and fall of the river. The path climbs steeply to the right, leaving the river and passing through beech woodland and beds of wild garlic.

Look out for a disused mine adit on the right-hand side.

As you leave the wood the track divides. Take the left branch level with the river bed.

The conifers ahead were planted just after the Second World War (Changing Woodland, see A7).

The path follows a bend in the river arriving at some old workings represented by a stone wall and river race. Beyond is a wooden bridge built by Norwegians and on the right are steps up the hillside signposted "Silica Mines". Another sign indicates "Gunpowder Works" across the bridge. Ignore these and continue along the river bed by a deep pool and scramble down to a weir below and on to the small island. This way is impassable when the river is in flood and a detour up and around to the right must be made, regaining the bank of the river further upstream. Continue along the path, now with an alder wood growing in a boggy area to your right, and cross a wooden stile.

The best time to visit this area is early morning when no-one else is around. This is when the woods are full of birdsong and you have your best chance of seeing dippers, herons and other birds along the streamcourse.

E4 Birds of the Waterfall Country - The fields, wooded slopes and river provide a wide variety of habitats for numerous birds. Lapwing are commonly seen in the valleys together with redshank and snipe. Birds found associated with woodland and along the river bank include breeding dipper, grey wagtail, goosander, pied flycatcher, redstart, wood warbler, woodcock, buzzard and sparrowhawk.

Shortly after the stile the river is forced into a much narrower channel with a number of small falls. Make a short detour here, dropping down left to explore these with a fine exposure of Millstone Grit in the opposite bank (see E5). The dip of the rocks to the south is clearly evident here. Above are numerous disused workings.

The path now climbs and then drops again to the river.

You can see old iron panels in the river bed and across on the opposite bank numerous old ruined stone buildings amongst conifers.

Continue to old stone piers at a former bridging point.

Explore this assortment of sluices and weirs which once provided the power for the gunpowder works here.

E4 Gunpowder Works - Alongside the Mellte was a gunpowder works which was unique in Wales at the time. The first owners were the Vale of Neath Powder Company but in 1862, Curtis and Harvey took over the works and eventually renamed it Nobels Explosives Company. In 1926 it became part of the Imperial Chemical Industries Limited. The site was understandably chosen for its isolation, the river supplied power and the woodland was used for making charcoal. The site covered about 180 acres stretching for nearly two miles. This meant that any explosion could be contained. The works are largely in ruins today but stonework and remnants of buildings can be seen, many of which have only three remaining walls as the fourth wall and roof were made of timber that would be blown off if an explosion occurred. The buildings were separated by banks of earth and many were whitewashed so that accumulation of gunpowder could be spotted easily. Workers wore special safety slippers made of leather and women were banned from wearing metal hairpins. Work commenced at 7.30 a.m. and nothing likely to cause a spark could be taken into the buildings. The gunpowder produced here was principally used in coal mines and quarries including the slate quarries of North Wales. The head of water that fed the water-wheels that powered the machinery was supplied via two weirs and a series of leats. Raw materials were hauled on a tramway by horses shod with copper shoes to prevent sparks.

---

7. From the weir, continue upstream past a small stone structure on the right to the first waterfall.

At the entrance to the pond below the fall the river has breached a band of Millstone Grit and the water actually runs down the dipslope of the bedding plane. The waterfall just beyond has been formed by a resistant band of sandstone.

Pass this fall up to the right, crossing a wide boulder-filled gully. There are good exposures in the right-hand wall of well-cleaved Millstone Grit. Leaving the gully, take the path that goes up to the right.

The gorge continues to narrow as you progress upstream with a steep drop from the path to the river. Both sides of the valley are wooded (Ancient Woodland, see E2).

Rounding the bend, the river straightens into a narrow channel with a number of small falls. The river then swings to the right around a spur of land. Eventually the path reaches a high point but do not descend where the path drops to river level. This is just before the river swings into a left-hand bend and the gorge further on soon becomes impassable. If you miss this point, retrace your steps to where the path reaches the crest of a small rise. At the high point on the path there is a steep grassy wooded slope leading up to the horizon. Make your way up this past an oak tree and keeping a small rock outcrop on the right-hand side. There is no clear path at first but keep on the arête of the hill meeting a path which zigzags upwards.

From here there are excellent views north of the interlocking spurs of this valley.

Continue east along a flattish section to a large oak tree on the left. East from here, a path leads along the side of a ditch on the left to a broken-down wall along the edge of a conifer plantation. The path swings to the right (with the wall on the left) through a cutting in the forestry to the high level path on the right which joins Sgwd yr Eira with Craig y Ddinas. Continue up the rise and cut off left at the route sign to Cilhepste-fach.

8. **Swing around the ruins and follow the wide path northwards. The path is parallel to the river which is well below.**

The Forestry Commission are attempting to regenerate oak woodland on the left of the path but have unfortunately decimated this area in previous years by draining the peat and heather moorland and planting alien conifers (Coniferous Forestry, see B5; Moorland

Under Threat, see D5).

Looking to the south-west is the Neath Valley with the land massif on the left, the Rhigos, forming the northern rim of the South Wales Coalfield. The rounded mountain straight ahead is Fan Nedd.

The path swings to the east and follows above the Afon Hepste to a group of large boulders and a footpath marker "Sgwd yr Eira" to the left and "Penderyn" to the right.

The sides of this gorge are very steep and, in fact, prevented the woodland here from being felled. This is an area of genuine "ancient woodland" which means that this is a completely natural habitat which has not been interfered with by man (see E2).

The group of four or five large boulders is a geological oddity as their rock type is not found in the National Park. They were, in fact, transported by glaciers during the Ice Age from much further afield and are known as "glacial erratics".

9. Drop steeply down wooden steps towards the river. Half way down the track divides. Take the right descending path which crosses behind the falls.

The gully you have just descended is where the geological fault runs, which was originally responsible for the creation of the fall. Passing behind the fall is one of the most memorable experiences in the National Park (see E3).

On the far bank keep down at river level, ignoring the path climbing the hillside by the steps.

Soon you come across a series of cascades called the Lower Cilhepste Falls. This is an exciting place to explore and to discover how these falls were formed.

E4 Lower Cilhepste Falls - This part of the gorge is where the Afon Hepste plunges over 70m down a number of steps to reach the confluence with the Afon Mellte. The Hepste gorge has been left as a "hanging valley" above the Mellte and these multiple cascades have been formed where the steepest gradient is found and where a geological fault crosses the gorge. This is the same fault which is responsible for Sgwd Isaf Clun-gwyn where it crosses the Mellte. The Mellte was able to "capture" the Hepste as its valley is much lower than the Hepste. This triggered a period of rapid erosion in the Hepste which is at its most active at these falls.

---

10. Strike up right, leaving the river path which soon becomes impassable. The path winds up in a zigzag past a rock boulder and a group of very tall beech trees on the left.

There is a choice of either taking an easy route which avoids a steep descent and an exposed path or a more adventurous route.

EASY OPTION - the easier option is to follow the main path which climbs above to the right to a spur above the confluence of the Hepste and the Mellte where there is a notice "Danger - Very steep rough slippery ground, deaths have occurred, take care". This is near to a large prominent oak tree. Head north from the notice, keeping to the top edge of the gorge.

HARD OPTION - if you are adventurous, and want to regain the bank of the river as soon as possible, keep left and contour round the spur on a shale path which drops down very steeply to the river. Use the trees and tree roots for safety here and arrive at the confluence of the Rivers Hepste and Mellte. Turn right (NW) up the River Mellte until the river bank becomes impassable and climb the spur on the right. Before reaching the top, take the path off to the left and traverse round the hillside, dropping to Sgwd y Pannwr. The path skirts just above the river and comes to a sign "Danger - very steep rocky path".

Rounding a right-hand bend in the gorge, you will hear the roar of a waterfall down in the gorge which is called Sgwd y Pannwr (Fall of the Fuller).

The slope on the right eases and the path drops gently through woodland, across a Millstone Grit boulder field to the waterfall.

11. Continue upstream along the river bank to the waterfall Sgwd Isaf Clyn-gwyn.

On your way to the waterfall, look to your right where there is a flat boggy area with alder woodland. The steep cliffs on the opposite bank in springtime will be covered in primroses. Just around the corner is another Millstone Grit boulder slope and beyond this is the most spectacular series of waterfalls in South Wales. Explore all the pools and cascades, savouring this very special place and learning about its formation (see E2).

Climb steeply above the last fall to the right of two large sandstone bands and take a slightly airy path along a terrace between these two massive bands of rock. This soon joins the main gorge path.

This exposed route provides an excellent aerial view of the fall below. The massive sandstone band above to your right is a very important geological feature and is known as the "twelve foot sandstone". Note the "mantel-shelf" that has formed at the base of this bed where the rock type changes to very weak, thinly bedded shales. This feature is responsible for many of the cascades in the Waterfall Country, none more noteworthy than Sgwd yr Eira.

Otherwise, cut up above this rock outcrop to the main high level path.

12. Proceed along the main high level path, around a bend in the gorge, to the next waterfall, Sgwd Clun-gwyn.

This side of the gorge provides the best high viewpoint of the waterfall and is an ideal spot from which to compose pictures. Look carefully at some of the loose boulders here to find a clue as to how the fall originally formed. Some of the rock surfaces have been polished and scored with parallel grooves. These are called "slickensides" and are formed when rocks grind together along a geological fault. These boulders are not, however, oriented in their original position when the earth movements occurred.

Climb to the gully that is in line with the waterfall.

The geological fault that formed the fall runs through this (Sgwd Clun-gwyn, see E2).

13. From here, either walk up to the wooden bridge, cross the river and follow the opposite bank down to the fall, or, to save time, descend to the river just above the fall and jump across at a narrow point.

The fall can be explored by climbing down its right edge to a rocky ledge half way down the fall. This is a good spot from which to take dramatic photographs. The deep pools above the fall are ideal for a refreshing dip on warm summer days. The ledge of the fall is a good place to learn more about its history (Sgwd Clun-gwyn, see E2).

From the top of the fall ascend the path up to the left through oak and hawthorn woodland. The track climbs more steeply to an open area and a gate by the renovated farmhouse of Clun-gwyn.

Cross the stile and over sheep grazing land to a second stile. Here there is a map of the Ystradfellte River system. Cross a small ford and up the track to the road.

14. Turn left (S) and walk back to the start.

E5. Afon Nedd/Afon Mellte River Walk

Start:	Pont Mellin-fach car park
Grid Reference:	9077 1050
Distance:	13km (8 miles)

This is a deceptively easy route which travels northwards along the banks of the Afon Nedd to one of the most interesting and impressive natural features in the area - Pwll-y-rhyd cave. The route then crosses into the Ystradfellte Valley over the limestone plateau and descends the Afon Mellte river past impressive waterfalls. The route is not well frequented, at least in its early stages, and can be quite difficult, especially in wet weather. There can be some problems in route finding as the path often leaves the river and the passage over the limestone plateau in the north requires good map reading. The geology of the valleys, moving from grit to limestone, is interesting and there is an Iron Age fort to the north.

* * *

ROUTE
1. Leave the car park to the north and cross over the bridge. Turn immediately left, cross over a stile and follow the path along the right bank of the stream signed to Pont Rhyd-y-cnau. The path drops to river level and, in a short distance, passes under a small cliff.

This may be difficult when the river is in flood and the stones are slippery. In these conditions this section may be passed at a higher level.

The path goes through hazel woodland with the odd oak on the flat area of river bank.

Look out for dippers and wagtails on the stream (Birds of the Waterfall Country, see E4).

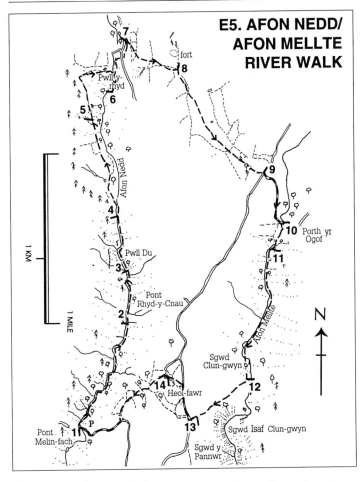

E5. AFON NEDD/ AFON MELLTE RIVER WALK

Eventually it becomes impossible to follow the path at river level and it skirts below the next set of crags climbing up to the top of the bank. Climb up to high level opposite this or the more adventurous can follow the narrow path behind the holly.

There is a pleasant plunging waterfall on the opposite bank. This

195

is a spectacular wooded area with boulders covered in a variety of mosses. The closer you stay to the edge, the more exciting or dangerous the walk becomes. The river takes a contorted route through steep gorge walls with the odd small waterfall and deep pool. The banks of the river are covered mainly with hazel, ash, holly, rowan and sycamore (Ancient Woodland, see E2).

The right of way marked on the map runs across the top of the cliff but the walk is more interesting when the bank is followed as far as conditions will allow.

Other tree species include silver birch and oak. The gorge walls were formed in the Millstone Grit and along this stretch you can see good examples of stratification.

E5 Geological rock formations of the Waterfall Country - Carboniferous Limestone was formed in warm, often clear shallow seas where corals, shellfish, brachiopods and crinoids (sea-lilies) were abundant. In fact, the skeletal remains of creatures such as these can make up much of the rock. The Devonian period ended when the southern flanks of St. George's Land subsided, resulting in the sea, which was confined to an area south of the present Bristol Channel, advancing northwards. This marked the beginning of Carboniferous times when up to 4000ft of grey calcareous shales and massive limestones were deposited. These rocks are divisible into three groups, Lower Limestone Shales, Main Limestone and Upper Limestone Shales, which reflect the establishment, hiatus and waning of a major marine cycle. These stable conditions were interrupted by earth movements caused by approaching continents from the west and south in mid-Carboniferous times which lifted the southern flanks of St. George's Land, resulting in a southward retreat of the sea. The rocks once laid down on the seabed were now exposed to erosion. Overlying the limestone is Millstone Grit which, in the Beacons, comprises in its lower layers massive white quartz conglomerates and sandstones, the Basal Grit. This group has very pure bands of over 99% quartz which were worked for fire-brick (silica brick). The Millstone Grit represents a marked change in depositional conditions to estuaries of large rivers in which fast currents carried coarse material eroded from mountains to the north. Many of the beds show rapid lateral changes from fine silty

---

muds to coarse sandstones, grits and conglomerates. These resistant layers are overlain by softer grey or blue shales and mudstones, the Middle Shales, which sometimes contain thin bands of coal. These shales are followed by massive beds of sandstone, known commonly by South Wales miners as the Farewell Rock as they knew that workable coal bands were left behind once they had struck this distinctive geological marker.

Follow your preferred route here, staying close to the river with a bit of scrambling across boulders and then strike up right to a stile. This is at grid line 11 on the map and there is a waterfall on the far river bank. Drop again to the river and continue north if water levels allow. Cross a small rivulet on the right and walk by a single strand fence.

This area is well populated with small woodland birds. Late April is a good time of the year to visit when all the woodland flowers are in bloom. Heron are commonly seen here.

Now and again fences have to be crossed by fairly rough stiles before coming to a sign to Pont Rhyd-y-cnau. Follow this to arrive at a concrete bridge with a gate barring the route.

Just below the bridge is a waterfall and there is a sloping block of Millstone Grit in the river bed which gives the true dip direction for the area.

2. Skirt past the bridge without crossing and continue through deciduous forestry along the river bank. Ignore the wide track down from the right to the bridge.

Dippers are quite common in the stream bed (Rivers of the Waterfall Country, see E2).

Continue on the west bank to the rapids through oak woodland and cross a stile and a stream gully. Fifty metres further is an impressive stepped waterfall on the far bank, which is spectacular when frozen. Part of the banks are composed of grit and part of limestone.

The trees on the river bank are covered in moss on the lower parts with a number of ferns growing from the trunks; these are called epiphytes. In the spring there is an abundance of woodland flowers including lesser celandine *(Ranunculus ficaria)*, a yellow flower.

Immediately past these waterfalls, the path enters a narrow gorge, and there is a river pool with a limestone cliff beyond it called **Pwll Du.**

The water here is extremely clear and flows out through the exit of the cave. This indicates that this pool is the resurgence of an underground cave system.

3. **Just after the pool, the path climbs up into a narrow gorge and up out of the right-hand side. Follow the path as it drops down below the crag. A short distance up from Pwll Du, the river swings to the right around a tall cliff. In the dry season you can traverse across the front of this, otherwise climb to the top.**

Above this point the resurgence of the river occurs. Water seeps out of the gravel-bed, having travelled underground leaving a dry river bed upstream. In spate, this phenomenon is obscured.

At the point where the dry river bed is between a narrow gorge, cut up right just before the crags on the path. Climb a grassy boulder incline up rock steps to large Millstone Grit boulders, and up to the fence on the top of the hillside.

On a still day, the gorge is peaceful and full of bird song.

Follow the path along the fence on the right. The path comes to a corner of the wire fence above which a stony track descends to the river. Follow this upstream to the bridge.

4. **Cross the bridge to the left bank and climb the farm track through coppiced hazel, passing the ruined building on the right of the path. The path bends to the left into a gully.**

This is worth a quick visit because it is headed by a sink hole over the lip of which fall several small streams which pass underground and eventually find their way down to the river.

Below the sink hole turn north through an ungated gap in the fence and into a field. Walk up this leaving a fence between you and the river far below in a deep gorge.

When ruined buildings come into view, head for these and follow the hawthorn hedge and the old wall to a stile. Cross this to the old farm buildings and up the track to join the Roman Road, Sarn Helen, at a sign which points back along this road and also back to Duffryn Nedd.

Clints and grykes in a limestone pavement that was once the site of a hill fort

5. Follow Sarn Helen along the edge of the coniferous forestry until just before two gates.

The hills ahead are Fan Nedd and the low bulk of Fan Gyhirych.

A track leaves on the right. Follow this stony road down to a gate where it bends to the left. On the bend, turn right off the track and cut down the river bank southwards to Pwll-y-rhyd which is about 100m downstream.

This is an incredible limestone sink hole, where the river pours over its lip and disappears for about 200m underground (Limestone, see E3).

The river can be crossed with care in dry conditions and the opposite bank can be explored.

6. If the river has been crossed, continue northwards up the eastern bank above Pwll-y-rhyd. Otherwise proceed upstream along the western bank to the bridge.

There is a choice of paths along the eastern bank, the lowest one passing below a cliff on rock steps in the river. This may need to be avoided in spate. The track now becomes sandy and arrives at a stile and bridge on the track you left before visiting Pwll-y-rhyd. There is a car park here.

Turn right up the tarmac track to a wider road and turn left by a sign for camping and caving.

7.   After about 150m cross a stile on the right of the road at a sign to Ystradfellte. Strike south-east diagonally across the field to a stile and then continue to hawthorn trees on the horizon. From these aim for the southern edge of the limestone hill fort, meeting and following a stone wall.

The fort is situated on a limestone pavement.

E5 Limestone pavement - Route E5 crosses one of the most southerly limestone pavements in Britain. The characteristic appearance results from the limestone, calcium carbonate, being dissolved along joints by slightly acidic rainwater. The raised blocks are known as clints and the clefts as grikes. In the past, this area was wooded as the plants found in the grikes are typical woodland species. The deep grikes have a stable "micro-climate" of low light levels and constant temperatures, characteristics of a woodland floor. Typical grike plant species include lily of the valley (Convallaria majalis), wall lettuce (Mycelis muralis), hard shield fern (Polystichum aculeatum), hairy rock-cress (Arabis hirsuta), brittle bladder fern (Cystopteris fragilis), limestone fern, globe flower (Trollius europaeus) and unusual limestone pavement species such as common cow-wheat (Melampyrum pratense), cowslip (Primula veris) and zigzag clover (Trifolium medium). Rarities include yellow archangel (Galebdolon luteum), found only in Wales, narrow-leaved bitter cress (Cardamine impatiens) and local drifts of mossy saxifrage (Saxifraga hypnoides). Dense hazel scrub is found in places with hawthorn, blackthorn, guelder-rose, dog rose, stone bramble, ivy, elder and honeysuckle.

---

8.   Cross over the stile and turn right, down the valley, to shortly meet a drovers' road. Follow this through an area of shake holes to

Resurgence of the Afon Mellte from Porth yr Ogof

the prominent Scots pines and then down the gully to meet the main road.

These pines mark the route of this old drovers' road (see D4).

9. Cross this and descend the narrow tarmac road to Porth yr Ogof.

There is a car park here, and the river north of the road bridge can be explored by dropping down a steep path from the car park. The river goes underground through Porth yr Ogof but don't be tempted to follow it as the cave has extremely deep and fast water courses.

10. From the car park, cross the bridge and turn left (S) over a stile and wander between limestone boulders and between two fenced-off sink holes in the depths of which can be heard the rushing river. The path descends to the eastern bank as the river emerges into a limestone gorge. The route can descend to the river here but an easier option stays above.

This pool is the resurgence of the Afon Mellte.

11. The path becomes easier and crosses above an open grassy area where the river is wider and more peaceful. After this is a stile which can be bypassed and there is a sign warning of dangerous paths and steep gorges. The path widens and runs close to the river through woodland. Cross a rivulet and the path meanders and climbs above the river, which has narrowed with rapids. There is a swing gate and the path is at river level.

This part of the walk is very popular, especially in summer, and can be quite congested.

Cross another small rivulet to a second swing gate and so to a sandy path curving left around the bend in the river to a wooden bridge with waymark arrows.

12. Cross the bridge and follow the clear path south to just above Sgwd Clun-gwyn waterfall.

You can detour down to the fall and explore it by climbing down the right edge to a rocky ledge half way down the fall. This is a good spot from which to take dramatic photographs (see E2).

Rejoin the path and ascend south-west following the track through bracken and oak and hawthorn woodland. The track climbs steeply at first to an open area and a gate by the renovated farmhouse of Clun-gwyn. Cross the stile and over sheep grazing land to a second stile. Here is a map of the Ystradfellte River system. Cross a small ford and up the track to the road.

13. Turn right (N) over a cattle grid and in 200m reach a shop and garage on the left and a phone booth on the right. Beyond is a small church (Capel Hermen) opposite which cross a stile, signed to Heol-fawr.

Strike across the field towards the farm hidden in the trees, and cross a waymarked stile turning right to a gate. Turn left on the road to Heol-fawr Farm.

14. Leaving this on your left, continue down a grassy track through a gate. Ignore the two farm tracks to your right and walk down an overgrown track which bends right then left to a white arrowed stile. Turn immediately right down a gully to a T-junction. Turn left and so to Glyn-mercher-uchaf Farm.

From the farm, join the road and turn right down to the bridge and back to the start.

Directions to the Starts of the Walks

SECTION A - STARTS OF WALKS

Llwynbedw, Cwm Llwch - start of walks A1, A2 and A3

From Brecon Town Centre.

1. Head west across the River Usk for 850m and take the second turning on the left (the first on the left is marked by a church). Drive along the Ffrwdgrech Road, passing under the Brecon by-pass and then on past an industrial estate on the right.
2. 1.2km from the underpass the road crosses a small bridge, Pont Ffrwd-grech, and soon afterwards splits into three.
3. Take the middle road, keeping right at a fork in the road after a further 1.1km.
4. Shortly after this the road drops into a small wooded valley and crosses a stream at Pont-rhyd-goch. Continue steeply up the other side and follow the road to a T-junction, 1.6km from the bridge.
5. Just to the right a farm track leads into the valley of Cwm Llwch. Follow this, passing through a gate after 1km which leads into a camping and parking field.

From Heads of the Valleys Road North of Merthyr

1. Leave the Heads of the Valleys Road, A465(T), by taking the A470(T) north, signposted Brecon. Drive north past three reservoirs on the left and over the pass to the village of Libanus.
2. Take the first turning on the right after passing the Mountains nursing home on the left. Cross the bridge over the Afon Tarell and at the T-junction at Libanus Mill turn right and follow the road for 150m to a sharp left bend. After the bend, climb gently and after 600m a road joins from the left. Drive straight on.
3. After 900m turn sharp left at a junction, dropping gently downhill and rise up the other side to a crossroads with a small lane on the left to a farm. Take the right turn for 300m to another crossroads. Turn right on a narrow road which soon becomes non-tarmac and

enters Cwm Llwch Valley. Travel on the rough road to a metal gate and so to the car park.

Pont y Caniedydd - start of walks A4, A5, A6, A7, A8 and A11

From Brecon Town Centre
1. Head west across the bridge over the River Usk and take the first turning on the left marked by a church with a spire on the far side of the junction.
2. This is called the Bailihelig Road and shortly comes to a mini-roundabout with a housing estate on the right. Carry straight on up the hill, passing a hospital on the right and then on over the Brecon by-pass.
3. Continue along this road, ignoring two left turns and one right, until it swings around to the left and comes to a T-junction, about 3.5km from the road bridge.
4. Turn right and down into a stream valley with a car parking area on the left just before the bridge, Pont y Caniedydd, across Nant Sere.

From Heads of the Valleys Road
1. Leave the Heads of the Valleys Road at the junction north of Merthyr and take the A470 north to the roundabout where the A470(T) meets the A40(T).
2. Leave the roundabout by the third exit signposted Brecon and then take the second turning on the right marked by a church with a spire on the near side of the junction.
3. From here follow points 2-4 above.

Near Rhiwiau - start for walks A9, A10 and A12
Suitable car parking is at a premium in this area and it may be necessary to park some distance from this starting point.

From Brecon Town Centre
1. Head east out of the town to a roundabout and take the second exit, the A40(T) east, and drive to the first turning on the left.
2. Take this, sweeping back on yourself, and turn left (south) along the B4558 back under the A40(T).
3. Cross over the Monmouthshire and Brecon Canal and then the River Usk. 500m from this bear right at a fork in the road and into

the village of Llanfrynach.

4. As you enter the built-up area bear right and right again. Follow the road around to the left, with the Afon (river) Cynrig down to the right. Shortly, bear left at a fork and 650m further on the road swings sharply right.

5. Take the lane straight ahead, ignoring two turnings on the left. The road climbs south up the hill ahead and reaches a dead end, just past the farm of Rhiwiau on the right and the white-washed cottage of Llyn Fron on the left.

From Heads of the Valleys Road

1. Take the A470(T) north to the roundabout west of Brecon and take the A40(T) east (fourth exit) to another roundabout.

2. Continue along the A40(T) east by taking the third exit.

3. From here follow points 2-5 above given from Brecon.

From Builth Wells on the A470(T)

1. Take the A470(T) south to the junction with the A40(T) east of Brecon. Leave the roundabout by the first exit along the A40(T) east.

2. From here follow points 2-5 above given from Brecon Town Centre.

From Crickhowell on the A40(T)

1. Take the A40(T) west past the village of Llanhamlach. After this the carriageways split for a short distance and a few hundred metres further on take a left turn and join the B4558 (south).

2. From here follow points 3-5 above given from Brecon Town Centre.

Near Tregaer - start for walks A13, A14 and A15

From Brecon Town Centre

1. Head east out of the town to a roundabout and take the second exit, the A40(T) east, and drive to the first turning on the left.

2. Take this, sweeping back on yourself, and turn left (south) along the B4558 back under the A40(T).

3. Cross over the Monmouthshire and Brecon Canal and then over the River Usk. 500m from this bear right at a fork in the road and into the village of Llanfrynach.

4. Bear left on entering the village, keeping the large church on the left. Follow round the Church Yard wall and at the apex of the bend take the road to the right past the telephone kiosk.
5. Cross over Llanfrynach Bridge and take the first turning on the right after 120m. There is a prominent sign here "Not Suitable for M.O.D. Vehicles".
6. Follow this up the hill for 700m to where a track on the right leaves to the farm of Tregaer and a number of farm gates encircle a small parking area on the left. No official car park exists here but suitable sites can be found on the verge further down the lane or in Llanfrynach village. **Under no circumstances should cars be left so that they impede farm machinery in any way.**

From Heads of the Valleys Road
1. Take the A470(T) north to the roundabout west of Brecon and take the A40(T) east (fourth exit) to another roundabout.
2. Continue along the A40(T) east by taking the third exit and drive to the first turning on the left.
3. From here follow points 2-6 above given from Brecon.

From Builth Wells on the A470(T)
1. Take the A470(T) south to the junction with the A40(T) east of Brecon. Leave the roundabout by the first exit along the A40(T) east and drive to the first turning on the left.
2. From here follow points 2-6 above given from Brecon.

From Crickhowell on the A40(T)
1. Leave the A40(T) east by following the signs to Talybont-on-Usk.
2. In the village turn right, north-west, along the B4558.
3. Just before the village of Pencelli bear left and then take the third lane on the left just before Llanfrynach village marked by a prominent sign, "Not Suitable for M.O.D. Vehicles".
4. Follow this up the hill for 700m to where a track on the right leaves to the farm of Tregaer and a number of farm gates encircle a small parking area on the left. No official car park exists here but suitable sites can be found on the verge further down the lane or in Llanfrynach village. **Under no circumstances should cars be left so that they impede farm machinery in any way.**

SECTION B - STARTS OF WALKS

Near Pencelli Church. Walk B1

From Brecon Town Centre
1. From the town centre head east along the B4601 to the roundabout and take the second exit, the A40(T) east.
2. Leave this at the first turning on the left, swinging back on yourself and turning left (south) along the B4558 back under the A40(T).
3. Follow this B road to Pencelli village (4km from the road junction). Pass the public house on the right and at the end of the village turn sharp right after crossing a bridge over the canal.
4. After 350m turn left up a narrow lane passing Plas Pencelli (an outdoor pursuits centre) on the right after 200m.
5. Continue up the road for about 500m to where the road opens out into a parking area opposite a church with a tower.

From Crickhowell on the A40(T)
1. Leave the A40(T) east by following the signs to Talybont-on-Usk.
2. In the village turn right, north-west, along the B4558.
3. Just before Pencelli village bear left and then take the first turning on the left up a narrow lane.
4. Follow point 5 above.

From Heads of the Valleys Road
1. Leave this road, the A465(T), by following the signs to the Brecon Mountain Railway. This junction is east of the A470(T) junction and west of the roundabout at Dowlais Top where there is a cafe and an Asda Superstore. Continue following signs to the Mountain Railway.
2. Continue on past the train station and take the second turning on the left. Cross the Taf Fechan river, and climb steeply into the village of Pontsticill. Turn right at the T-junction and drive north.
3. Pass the Ponsticill reservoir on the right and towards the end of this turn sharp left up a steep hill, ignoring the road which continues straight on and over the dam.
4. Just past the next reservoir turn right and down a hill following the signs to Talybont.

5. The road now climbs steeply to a pass and drops down a severe gradient into the Talybont Valley. It is not surprising that this stretch often becomes impassable in wintry conditions.
6. Drive past the Talybont reservoir on the right and over the swingbridge across the Monmouthshire and Brecon Canal, just before the village of Talybont-on-Usk.
7. Do not go into the village but turn left and head north-west on the B4558 towards the village of Pencelli.
8. Just before the village bear left and take the first turning up a narrow lane.
9. Continue up the road for about 500m to where the road opens out into a parking area opposite a church with a tower.

Talybont Reservoir Car Park. Walk B2

From Brecon
1. Head east along the B4601 to a roundabout and take the second exit, the A40(T) east.
2. Continue along this passing through the village of Llanhamlach and at the small village of Llansantffraed turn right, just past a church with a spire on the left. The road is signposted to Talybont-on-Usk.
3. At the T-junction in the village turn right, go through the village and then turn left crossing a swingbridge over the Monmouthshire and Brecon Canal.
4. Follow this road through Aber village and after passing the reservoir dam on the left, turn left after 1km into a car park.

From Crickhowell on the A40(T)
1. Driving west along the A40(T) from the direction of Crickhowell turn left just before the village of Llansantffraed, signposted Talybont-on-Usk, to a T-junction.
2. At the T-junction in the village turn right, go through the village and turn left crossing a swingbridge over the Monmouthshire and Brecon Canal.
3. Follow this road through Aber village and continue past the reservoir dam on the left. After 1km enter a park on your left.

From the Heads of the Valleys Road
1. Leave this road, the A465(T), by following the signs to the Brecon Mountain Railway. This junction is east of the A470(T) junction and west of the roundabout at Dowlais Top where there is a cafe and an Asda Superstore.
2. Continue on past the train station and take the second turning on the right, cross the Taf Fechan river, and climb steeply into the village of Pontsticill. Turn right at the T-junction and drive north.
3. Pass the Ponsticill reservoir on the right and towards the end of this turn sharp left up a steep hill, ignoring the road which continues straight on and over the dam.
4. Just past the next reservoir turn right and down a hill following the signs to Talybont.
5. The road now climbs steeply to a pass and drops down a severe gradient into the Talybont Valley. It is not surprising that this stretch often becomes impassable in wintry conditions.
6. Towards the end of the Talybont reservoir look for a car parking area on the right in an area of coniferous forestry. The conifer plantation on the left finishes just before this point.

Forestry Commission Car Park, Pont Blaen-y-glyn. Walks B3 & B4

From Breco
1. Follow the directions given from Brecon to the Talybont reservoir car park (Walk B2).
2. Continue past this car park and drive south up the Talybont Valley, past the reservoir on the left, to the bridge over the Caerfanell river.
3. Just past this up on the left is a Forestry Commission gravel track which widens after a while into a car park.

From Crickhowell on the A40(T)
1. Follow the directions given from the A40(T) to the Talybont reservoir car park (Walk B2).
2. Then follow points 2-3 above.

From the Heads of the Valleys Road
1. Follow the directions given for the Heads of the Valleys road to the Talybont reservoir, but only follow as far as points 1-5.

2. Towards the bottom of the steep hill a Forestry Track leads off to the right, just before the bridge over the Caerfanell. There is a large car park here.

Talybont Torpantau car park. Walk B5

From Brecon Town Centre
1. Make your way to the Pont Blaen-y-glyn Forestry car park (described under Walk B3).
2. Drive past this and climb the steep long hill to the tight bends near the top, just after which a right turn leads into the Talybont Torpantau Forestry Commission car park.

From Crickhowell on the A40(T)
1. Follow directions given from the A40(T) (Walks B3 and B4) to the Pont Blaen-y-glyn Forestry car park.
2. Drive past this and climb the steep long hill to the tight bends near the top, just after which a right turn leads into the Talybont Torpantau Forestry Commission car park.

From the Heads of the Valleys Road
1. Leave this road, the A465(T), by following the signs to the Brecon Mountain Railway. This junction is east of the A470(T) junction and west of the roundabout at Dowlais Top where there is a cafe and an Asda Superstore.
2. Continue on past the train station and take the second turning on the right, cross the Taf Fechan river, and climb steeply into the village of Pontsticill. Turn right at the T-junction and drive north.
3. Pass the Ponsticill reservoir on the right and towards the end of this turn sharp left up a steep hill, ignoring the road which continues straight on and over the dam.
4. Cross the Taf Fechan river and climb steeply to the highest point of the pass.
5. Just as the road begins to descend turn left into a Forestry Commission car park, before some tight bends. Drive a few hundred metres to a cattle grid and over on the right-hand side is a Forestry Commission sign saying Talybont Torpantau.

SECTION C - STARTS OF WALKS

Taf Fechan Forestry Commission car park. Walk C1

From Brecon Town Centre

1. Head east along the B4601 to a roundabout and take the second exit, the A40(T) east.
2. Continue along this passing through the village of Llanhamlach and at the small village of Llansantffraed turn right, just past a church with a spire on the left, signposted Talybont-on-Usk.
3. At the T-junction turn right, go through the village and turn left, crossing a swingbridge over the Monmouthshire and Brecon Canal.
4. Drive along the Talybont Valley and over the pass to a T-junction.
5. Turn right, signposted Neuadd reservoir and drive north-west into the Taf Fechan Valley.
6. Cross a bridge after 1km, ignore a car park on the right and continue 1.5km to another on the left, situated in a Forestry Commission conifer plantation.

From Crickhowell on the A40(T)

1. Driving west along the A40(T) from the direction of Crickhowell turn left just before the village of Llansantffraed, signposted Talybont-on-Usk.
2. Follow directions 3-6 given above to the Blaen Taf Fechan Forestry Commission car park below the Neuadd reservoirs.

From the Heads of the Valleys Road

1. Leave this road, the A465(T), by following the signs to the Brecon Mountain Railway. This junction is east of the A470(T) junction and west of the roundabout at Dowlais Top where there is a cafe and an Asda Superstore.
2. Continue on past the train station and take the second turning on the left, cross the Taf Fechan river, and climb steeply into the village of Pontsticill. Turn right at the T-junction and drive north.
3. Pass the Ponsticill reservoir on the right and towards the end of this turn sharp left up a steep hill, ignoring the road which continues straight on and over the dam.
4. Just past the next reservoir carry straight on following the sign to

the Neuadd reservoirs.

5. Cross a bridge after 1km, ignore a car park on the right and continue 1.5km to another on the left, situated in a Forestry Commission conifer plantation.

Pont Nant Gwinau. Walk C2

From Brecon

1. Leave Brecon by the B4601 west, over the River Usk, to the roundabout.
2. Take the A470(T) south (second exit), signposted Merthyr, and drive south-west through the village of Libanus.
3. Continue over the pass and descend the other side past the Beacons reservoir.
4. About 2km past the A4059 turning on the right, the road passes over Nant Crew Bridge, with the head of the Cantref reservoir on the right.
5. Continue south for a further 4km until reaching the next reservoir (Llwyn-on). Park on a disused stretch of old road on the left where the stream passes under the road.

From the Heads of the Valleys Road

1. Leave the Heads of the Valleys Road by taking the A470(T) north, signposted Brecon.
2. At the head of the first reservoir on the left (Llwyn-on), parking places can be found on the right on a stretch of old disused road.

From Crickhowell on the A40(T)

1. Continue on this road, by-passing Brecon to the roundabout west of the town.
2. From the roundabout follow points 2-5 as given from Brecon to Pont Nant Gwinau.

Northern Corner of Forestry Commission Plantation on A470. Walk C3

From Brecon

1. Follow the directions 1-4 (Walk C2) given from Brecon to Nant Crew Bridge. Having looked at the view from the bridge, retrace northwards for 1km and park on the left-hand verge opposite the

northern corner of the forestry plantation.

From Crickhowell on the A40(T)
1. Continue on this road, by-passing Brecon, to the roundabout west of the town.
2. Take the A470 to Nant Crew Bridge following points 2-4 in the directions from Brecon in Walk C2.
3. After looking at the view from Nant Crew Bridge retrace northwards back towards Brecon and park on the left-hand verge opposite the northern corner of the forestry plantation.

From the Heads of the Valleys Road
1. Leave the Heads of the Valleys Road by taking the A470(T) north, signposted Brecon.
2. Continue past the first reservoir, Llwyn-on, to the second (Cantref) and stop at Nant Crew Bridge at its northern end.
3. After looking at the view from here, continue northwards towards Brecon for 1km and park on the left-hand verge opposite the northern corner of the forestry plantation.

SECTION D - STARTS OF WALKS

Lay-by on A470(T). Walk D1

From Brecon Town Centre
1. Leave Brecon on the B4601 west, over the River Usk, to the roundabout.
2. Take the A470(T) south (second exit), signposted Merthyr, and drive south-west, passing through the village of Libanus.
3. Continue past the right turning for the A4215 for about 3.5km where there is a lay-by on the right and shortly afterwards there is another at the entrance to a cwm. Park in the second lay-by.

From Crickhowell on the A40(T)
1. Continue on this road from the direction of Crickhowell to the roundabout west of Brecon.
2. Follow points 2-3 above.

From the Heads of the Valleys Road
1. Leave the A465(T) by taking the A470(T) north signposted Brecon. Drive north past three reservoirs and over the pass where there is the Storey Arms centre, a white building on the right.
2. About 3km further on there is a lay-by on the left. Park here. There is a picnic area on the other side of the fence at the entrance to a steep-sided cwm.

Lay-by off A4059. Walk D2

1. Leave Brecon on the B4601 west, over the River Usk, to the roundabout.
2. Take the A470(T) south (second exit), signposted Merthyr, and drive south-west, passing through the village of Libanus.
3. Drive over the pass and continue to the end of the Beacons reservoir (first reservoir) where the A4059 leaves to the right.
4. Take this and cross over the bridge, around the sharp left-hand bend and stop after about 750m, finding a suitable place to park just off the road. There is a small lay-by south of where the stream crosses under the road at Nant yr Eira bridge.

From Crickhowell on the A40(T)

1. Continue on this road from the direction of Crickhowell to the roundabout west of Brecon.
2. Take the first exit, the A470(T) south, signposted Merthyr.
3. Follow points 3-4 above.

From the Heads of the Valleys Road

1. Leave the A465(T) by taking the A470(T) north, signposted Brecon. Drive north past two reservoirs and turn left just before the third, on the A4059.
2. Cross over the bridge, around the sharp left-hand bend, and stop after about 750m, finding a suitable place to park just off the road. There is a small lay-by south of where the stream crosses under the road at Nant yr Eira bridge.

Near Forest Lodge Cottages. Walk D3

From Brecon Town Centre

1. Leave Brecon on the B4601 west, over the river Usk, to the roundabout.
2. Take the A470(T) south, signposted Merthyr, and drive south-west, passing through the village of Libanus.
3. 1km after Libanus turn right on the A4215.
4. Ignore the first turning on the left and take the second on the left 2km after leaving the A470(T).
5. At a sharp right bend (Forest Lodge Cottages) there is space to park along the verge but make sure any farm machinery can pass with ease.

From Crickhowell on the A40(T)

1. Continue on this road from the direction of Crickhowell to the roundabout west of Brecon.
2. Follow points 2-5 in the directions from Brecon Town Centre.

From the Heads of the Valleys Road

1. Leave the A465(T) by taking the A470(T) north, signposted Brecon. Drive north past three reservoirs on the left and over the pass where there is the Storey Arms centre, a white building on the right.

2. After 5km turn back sharp left on the A4215.
3. Follow points 4-5 in the directions from Brecon Town Centre.

Sarn Helen. Walk D4

From Brecon Town Centre

1. Leave Brecon on the B4601 west, over the River Usk, to the roundabout.
2. Take the A470(T) south, signposted Merthyr, and drive south-west, passing through the village of Libanus.
3. 1km after Libanus turn right along the A4215. Drive for 3.5km, ignoring two turnings on the left to where the A4215 swings to the right and two roads leave to the left. Take the second which runs straight ahead.
4. Continue for 2.5km and turn left, signposted Ystradfellte, and drive south along the Senni Valley. The road climbs steeply up the left side with two very sharp bends, a popular stopping place for views of the Senni Valley. Continue for 1.2km to where the road bends to the right where a stony track leaves to the left.

From Crickhowell on the A40(T)

1. Continue on this road from the direction of Crickhowell to the roundabout west of Brecon.
2. Follow points 2-4 above.

From the Heads of the Valleys Road A465(T)

1. Leave this at a junction near Hirwaun by taking the A4059, signposted Brecon.
2. Pass through Penderyn village and 1.5km further on turn left, signposted Ystradfellte.
3. At the next Y-junction bear right and carry straight on to Castell Mellte, cross over the stream and turn right at the T-junction.
4. Follow this road for about 5km to where the road bends to the left and a stony track carries straight on.

Walk D5

Same as for D4 but the start is 0.6km north along the road, just before Maen Llia, a standing stone.

SECTION E - STARTS OF WALKS

Pontneddfechan. Walks E1 and E2

From Brecon

1. Leave Brecon on the B4601 west, over the River Usk, to the roundabout.
2. Take the A470(T) south, signposted Merthyr, drive up the valley, over the pass and turn right after the Beacons reservoir along the A4059.
3. After about 10km turn right, signposted Ystradfellte, and at the next junction bear left, again signposted Ystradfellte.
4. Turn left again 1km further on, this turning being quite easy to miss.
5. Follow this narrow lane into the valley, across the river and turn left at the T-junction on the other side.
6. Drive south for 7km to Pontneddfechan. At the bottom of the hill turn right and then right again between a row of cottages with the Old White Horse pub on the right. There is an information centre in the village.

From Crickhowell on the A40(T) east

1. At the roundabout west of Brecon follow points 2-6 above.

From the Heads of the Valleys Road

1. Leave the A465(T) by taking the A4109, the Inter-Valley Road, to the traffic lights in Glyn-neath.
2. Turn right here and then turn left onto the B4242, signposted Pontneddfechan.
3. Pass the information centre on the right, cross over the bridge and turn left between a row of cottages with the Old White Horse pub on the right.

Penderyn. Walk E3

From Brecon

1. Leave Brecon on the B4601 west, over the River Usk, to the roundabout.
2. Take the A470(T) south, signposted Merthyr, drive up the valley, over the pass and turn right after the Beacons reservoir along the

A4059.
3. Continue along this to Penderyn. Just before the start of the village turn right and 100m later a road leaves to the left. Park in a suitable place near to this junction.

From Crickhowell on the A40(T) east
1. At the roundabout west of Brecon follow points 2-3 above.

From the Heads of the Valleys Road
1. Leave the A465(T) at Hirwaun by taking the A4059, signposted Brecon, to the village of Penderyn.
2. From the start of the built-up area take the second turning on the left and 200m further on there is a T-junction. Park in a suitable place near to this.

Coed y Rhaiadr Forestry Car Park. Walk E4

From Brecon
1. Follow the same route as if you were going to Pontneddfechan for walks E1 and E2.
2. About 3km south of the youth hostel (which is about 2km south of Ystradfellte village) is a Forestry Commission car park on the left called Coed y Rhaiadr.

From the Heads of the Valleys Road
1. Follow the same route as for Pont Melin-fach (Walk E5 below) but where the single electricity cable crosses the road, do not turn left to Pont Melin-fach, but drive 300m to the car park (Forestry Commission Coed y Rhaiadr) on the right.

Pont Melin-fach. Walk E5

From Brecon
1. Leave Brecon on the B4601 west, over the River Usk, to the roundabout.
2. Take the A470(T) south, signposted Merthyr, drive up the valley, over the pass and turn right after the Beacons reservoir along the A4059.
3. After about 10km turn back sharp right, signposted Ystradfellte, and at the next junction turn left, again signposted Ystradfellte.

4. Turn left again 1km further on, this turning being quite easy to miss.

5. Follow this narrow lane into the valley to Porth yr Ogof where there is a car park. Cross the river and turn left at the T-junction on the other side.

6. Drive for 4km, past a youth hostel, garage and a turning on the right and take the next right.

7. Follow this to a bridge across a river, Pont Melin-fach, to a parking area on the other side of the bridge to the left.

From A40(T) east

1. At the roundabout west of Brecon follow points 2-7 above.

From the Heads of the Valleys Road

1. Leave the Heads of the Valleys road (A465T) and pass under the bridge (A4109). At the traffic lights turn right onto the road signposted to Pontneddfechan and the Rhigos (B4242).

2. In a few hundred metres, bear left at a signpost for Pontneddfechan (B4242) and the waterfalls (brown sign). Drive into Pontneddfechan village, pass the information centre on the right, over the river and to the Craig y Ddinas hotel through the village.

3. Follow the road up to the left, signposted Ystradfellte 4$^{1}/_{2}$ miles. The road climbs through the housing estate, crosses a cattle grid and onto the open moor.

4. Turn left where a single strand power line crosses the road and there is a wooden sign to Pont Melin-fach. Follow the narrow road down to a bridge over which is the Coed y Rhaiadr Pont Melin-fach Forestry Commission car park. There is quite a large picnic area to the south.

APPENDIX 2:
Useful Addresses

Brecon Beacons National Park
Office
7 Glamorgan Street
Brecon
Powys LD3 7DP
Tel: 01874 624437

Brecon Beacons Mountain Centre
near Libanus
Brecon
Powys LD3 8ER
Tel: 01874 623366

Brecknock Wildlife Trust
Lion House
Lion Street
Brecon
Tel: 01874 625708

National Trust
King's Head
1 Bridge Street
Llandeilo
Dyfed SA19 6BN
Tel: 01558 822800

Countryside Council for Wales
South Wales Regional Office
43 The Parade
Roath
Cardiff CF2 3AB
Tel: 01222 485111

Wales Tourist Board
Brunel House
Fitzalan Road
Cardiff
Tel: 01222 499909

CICERONE GUIDES
Cicerone publish a wide range of reliable guides to walking and climbing in Britain, and other general interest books.

LAKE DISTRICT - General Books
CONISTON COPPER A History
CHRONICLES OF MILNTHORPE
A DREAM OF EDEN -LAKELAND DALES
EDEN TAPESTRY
THE HIGH FELLS OF LAKELAND
LAKELAND - A taste to remember (Recipes)
LAKELAND VILLAGES
LAKELAND TOWNS
THE LAKERS
THE LOST RESORT? (Morecambe)
LOST LANCASHIRE (Furness area)
OUR CUMBRIA Stories of Cumbrian Men and Women
THE PRIORY OF CARTMEL
REFLECTIONS ON THE LAKES
AN ILLUSTRATED COMPANION INTO LAKELAND

LAKE DISTRICT - Guide Books
THE BORDERS OF LAKELAND
BIRDS OF MORECAMBE BAY
CASTLES IN CUMBRIA
CONISTON COPPER MINES Field Guide
THE CUMBRIA CYCLE WAY
THE EDEN WAY
IN SEARCH OF WESTMORLAND
SHORT WALKS IN LAKELND-1: SOUTH LAKELAND
SCRAMBLES IN THE LAKE DISTRICT
MORE SCRAMBLES IN THE LAKE DISTRICT
THE TARNS OF LAKELAND VOL 1 - WEST
WALKING ROUND THE LAKES
WALKS IN SILVERDALE/ARNSIDE
WESTMORLAND HERITAGE WALK
WINTER CLIMBS IN THE LAKE DISTRICT

NORTHERN ENGLAND (outside the Lakes
BIRDWATCHING ON MERSEYSIDE
CANAL WALKS Vol 1 North
CANOEISTS GUIDE TO THE NORTH EAST
THE CLEVELAND WAY & MISSING LINK
THE DALES WAY
DOUGLAS VALLEY WAY
WALKING IN THE FOREST OF BOWLAND
HADRIANS WALL VOL 1 The Wall Walk
HERITAGE TRAILS IN NW ENGLAND
THE ISLE OF MAN COASTAL PATH
THE LANCASTER CANAL
LANCASTER CANAL WALKS
A WALKERS GUIDE TO THE LANCASTER CANAL
LAUGHS ALONG THE PENNINE WAY
A NORTHERN COAST-TO-COAST
NORTH YORK MOORS Walks
THE REIVERS WAY (Northumberland)
THE RIBBLE WAY
ROCK CLIMBS LANCASHIRE & NW
WALKING DOWN THE LUNE
WALKING IN THE SOUTH PENNINES
WALKING IN THE NORTH PENNINES
WALKING IN THE WOLDS
WALKS IN THE YORKSHIRE DALES (3 VOL)
WALKS IN LANCASHIRE WITCH COUNTRY
WALKS IN THE NORTH YORK MOORS (2 VOL)
WALKS TO YORKSHIRE WATERFALLS (2 vol)
WATERFALL WALKS -TEESDALE & THE HIGH PENNINES
WALKS ON THE WEST PENNINE MOORS
WALKING NORTHERN RAILWAYS (2 vol)
THE YORKSHIRE DALES A walker's guide

Also a full range of EUROPEAN and OVERSEAS guidebooks - walking, long distance trails, scrambling, ice-climbing, rock climbing.

DERBYSHIRE & EAST MIDLANDS
KINDER LOG
HIGH PEAK WALKS
WHITE PEAK WAY
WHITE PEAK WALKS - 2 Vols
WEEKEND WALKS IN THE PEAK DISTRICT
THE VIKING WAY
THE DEVIL'S MILL / WHISTLING CLOUGH (Novels)

WALES & WEST MIDLANDS
ASCENT OF SNOWDON
WALKING IN CHESHIRE
CLWYD ROCK
HEREFORD & THE WYE VALLEY A Walker's Guide
HILLWALKING IN SNOWDONIA
HILL WALKING IN WALES (2 Vols)
THE MOUNTAINS OF ENGLAND & WALES Vol 1 WALES
WALKING OFFA'S DYKE PATH
THE RIDGES OF SNOWDONIA
ROCK CLIMBS IN WEST MIDLANDS
SARN HELEN Walking Roman Road
SCRAMBLES IN SNOWDONIA
SEVERN WALKS
THE SHROPSHIRE HILLS A Walker's Guide
SNOWDONIA WHITE WATER SEA & SURF
WALKING DOWN THE WYE
WELSH WINTER CLIMBS

SOUTH & SOUTH WEST ENGLAND
WALKING IN THE CHILTERNS
COTSWOLD WAY
COTSWOLD WALKS (3 VOLS)
WALKING ON DARTMOOR
WALKERS GUIDE TO DARTMOOR PUBS
EXMOOR & THE QUANTOCKS
THE KENNET & AVON WALK
LONDON THEME WALKS
AN OXBRIDGE WALK
A SOUTHERN COUNTIES BIKE GUIDE
THE SOUTHERN-COAST-TO-COAST
SOUTH DOWNS WAY & DOWNS LINK
SOUTH WEST WAY - 2 Vol
THE TWO MOORS WAY Dartmoor-Exmoor
WALKS IN KENT Bk 2
THE WEALDWAY & VANGUARD WAY

SCOTLAND
THE BORDER COUNTRY - WALKERS GUIDE
BORDER PUBS & INNS A Walker's Guide
CAIRNGORMS WINTER CLIMBS
WALKING THE GALLOWAY HILLS
THE ISLAND OF RHUM
THE SCOTTISH GLENS (Mountainbike Guide)
  Book 1:THE CAIRNGORM GLENS
  Book 2 THE ATHOLL GLENS
  Book 3 THE GLENS OF RANNOCH
SCOTTISH RAILWAY WALKS
SCRAMBLES IN LOCHABER
SCRAMBLES IN SKYE
SKI TOURING IN SCOTLAND
TORRIDON A Walker's Guide
WALKS from the WEST HIGHLAND RAILWAY
WINTER CLIMBS BEN NEVIS & GLENCOE

REGIONAL BOOKS UK & IRELAND
THE ALTERNATIVE PENNINE WAY
CANAL WALKS Vol.1: North
LIMESTONE - 100 BEST CLIMBS
THE PACKHORSE BRIDGES OF ENGLAND
THE RELATIVE HILLS OF BRITAIN
THE MOUNTAINS OF ENGLAND & WALES
  VOL 1 WALES, VOL 2 ENGLAND
THE MOUNTAINS OF IRELAND

Other guides are constantly being added to the Cicerone List.
Available from bookshops, outdoor equipment shops or direct (send s.a.e. for price list) from
CICERONE, 2 POLICE SQUARE, MILNTHORPE, CUMBRIA, LA7 7PY

PRNTED BY
CARNMOR PRINT & DESIGN, PRESTON, U.K.